Nature at Night

Finding Faith,
Wonder,
& Resilience
After Dark

Laurie Kehler

Nature at Night
Copyright ©2025 Laurie Ostby Kehler
Published by Brookmill House Publishing

ISBN: 979-8-9901282-0-0

All illustrations are by the author

Subjects: Nature–Religious aspects–Christianity–Meditations
Creation–Meditations | Spirituality–Christianity

Other books by the author
Gardening Mercies – Finding God in Your Garden
This Outside Life – Finding God in the Heart of Nature
Wings of Mercy – Spiritual Reflections from the Birds of the Air

For my beloved son Jack-
Fellow night owl and editor of excellence

"Look deep into nature, and then you will understand everything better."

Albert Einstein

"But ask the animals, and they will teach you, or the birds in the sky, and they will tell you; or speak to the earth, and it will teach you, or let the fish in the sea inform you. Which of these does not know that the hand of the Lord has done this? In his hand is the life of every creature and the breath of all mankind."

Job 12:7-10

Contents

For free nighttime resources visit:

www.LaurieKehler.com/nightresources

For nature-related gifts and products visit:

www.TheNatureOfHopeShop.com

CHAPTER 1

Sea Otter

U nder navy velvet skies spangled with the Milky Way and Orion, the gentle ocean waves lift the swaying fronds and blades of the giant kelp beds off the Monterey coast. The giant kelp plunges down 130 feet below the surface and is anchored to the rocky bottom by a spaghetti-like structure called a holdfast. Kelp is not a plant because it does not use roots to absorb nutrients, but it is one of the fastest-growing autotrophs—organisms that produce food from sunlight on the planet. Given the right conditions, giant kelp can grow nearly 2 feet a day.

These "liquid forests" that undulate and sway with the ocean swells provide a rich biodiverse habitat for thousands of species, both microscopic and substantial. Surging schools of silver jack mackerel, bright-orange garibaldi, and rockfish are abundant here. Spiny lobsters, abalone, crabs, shrimps, and sea urchins skitter and mince down the stalks and across the rocky bottom. Millions of microscopic animals cluster about the swaying leaves—or blades—and call the kelp forests home. Seals and sea lions dart, play, and hunt in their shadowy emerald depths.

And on the surface, wrapped up like presents in the bobbing and swaying fronds are one of the world's cutest and most endearing creatures, the sea otter.

The fact that any sea otters are still living is a minor miracle. Once plentiful and common from Alaska down to Baja California, they were hunted nearly to extinction for their remarkable fur. Sadly, the Oregon coast has never recovered its sea otter population; they've been completely wiped out.

Why were they hunted so voraciously? The sea otters' fur is the densest animal fur on the planet, which is why they were prized for their pelts. Nearly one million hairs per square inch is what keeps them warm. They do not have blubber like whales or seals, so they spend a lot of time grooming and keeping their fur clean by untangling knots, rubbing the coat to squeeze out excess water and blowing air directly into their fur. Keeping the fur well-groomed is the key to keeping them warm and buoyant in the frigid waters.

But even now, in their "safe" places, they are under threat from pollution, flushed kitty litter, and many diseases. (Feline feces carries a parasite—*toxoplasma gondii*—that is toxic to otters). Oil spills are catastrophic to their fur's insulation abilities, and without intervention, they can die of hypothermia. Thankfully, there is now more awareness and protection for them. Scientists have discovered sea otters' vital role in maintaining kelp forests and all the creatures that live in them. Without sea otters, sea urchins overpopulate the sea floor and decimate the kelp forests that provide cover and food for thousands of marine animals. This is why the otters are recognized as a "keystone species" in the ecosystem.

And they can eat an amazing amount of food. Sea otters eat 25 to 30 percent of their body weight in one day, which is like a 175-pound person eating 45 pounds of food in a day. Unperturbed by the purple, spiky barbs, they love sea urchins, as well as clams, mussels, and crabs. But how do they crack open those hard shells?

Unlike seagulls or squirrels, who have figured out that dropping shells and nuts onto hard surfaces will crack them open, sea otters are among the few animals that use tools. They dive down to collect a rock, swim up to the surface, float on their backs, and then begin striking their future meal with the rock until it opens.

It's not just use of tools that separate sea otters from otters you find in fresh water or rivers and streams. Sea otters grow to about five feet long and 100 pounds. That's two to three times the size of river otters. Ocean-dwelling otters also always float on their backs—belly up—as opposed to the river otters' belly down position. Finally, river otters live most of their lives on solid ground and sleep in dens and use the water for travel and food. The sea otters spend most of their lives in the water where they breed, give birth, forage, and sleep.

And that's where the supremely charming part of sea otters comes into focus. How they sleep. Because they spend all their time in the water, they are at the mercy of the waves and currents of the ocean. So, our sea otter does two things to combat the pull of the ocean: she rolls and wraps herself in the long fronds of giant kelp, which helps her stay put and not drift away. She wraps up her babies as well while she hunts for food so they don't get lost. And perhaps the most charming behavior of all, sea otters *hold hands* with others while they sleep.

While we are hoping to drift off to sleep as the stars dance across the skies, our furry friends are bobbing on the ocean swells and holding hands to prevent them from drifting off to sea. To leave the safety of the kelp beds means getting attacked by predators or maybe losing your mate to another. So, otter families and mates will lie back under the stars, floating above the swells and kelp beds, and sleep holding hands. The world may be in a tumult, wars and rumors of wars may crackle in the airwaves, and sharks might be lurking outside the kelp beds. But each evening they lean back, face the heavens, and reach out and hold each other close.

This is something we can do too. While nations and economies swell and ebb, while storms batter our lives, and danger that we have no control over lurks on the edges, we have the sea otter to remind us that it's a good idea to hold hands. Now more than ever, we need to hold our loved ones close.

Holding hands is an underappreciated but powerful gesture. I first fell in love with my husband because of this.

On our first date I took him to a Friday night church service that would provide him with the bluesy, gospel, enthusiastic worship I knew he would enjoy. As we stood there enjoying the music, he reached out and held my hand. It wasn't a limp hand, it wasn't cold, nor clammy (ugh!). But a strong, self-assured, warm grasp that my whole body resonated with as "coming home."

Hand-holding is sweeter than an arm around the shoulders. Too often, this transmits "my territory" or, "my possession." Or sometimes, the communication is, "I hope there's something more later." Holding someone's hand says in a kind, reassuring way, "We are side-by-side in this. I am here for you. Traveling through life together as partners and sojourners."

My mother first taught me the secret hand-holding language when I was younger. She would squeeze my hand three times in succession. That meant, "I-love-you." I was supposed to squeeze back four times: "I-love-you-too." Then the fun part, two squeezes: *"How-much?"* Then it was on! The person demonstrating their love squeezed the recipient's hand as hard as they could stand it.

Sometimes, I reach over to my ginormous, 6'3" son who doesn't go for big demonstrations of emotion with a knee squeeze: 1-2-3. I know he knows I'm saying, "I-love-you."

When my mother was just weeks from passing away from cancer, I was holding her hand, thinking of those days in my childhood when we would 1-2-3 squeeze I-love-you to each other. I quickly took a picture. "Why on earth are you taking a picture of these old things?" she asked. True, her hands were no longer youthful and elegant. At 83 her knuckles were enlarged with arthritis, ropy blue veins transversed the backs, and age spots covered the rest. But to me, my mother's hands were beautiful. They fed me my first food. They put a soothing washcloth on my forehead when I was sick. They taught me to pray. They cheered and clapped at my swimming races. They gave food to the needy, created thoughtful gardens for the blind, and served willingly. As I held her hand, I could only hope my hands accomplished as much.

When we are on a plane, as we are taking off, my husband and I silently reach over and hold each other's hands. We know what we are both doing. We are praying. Praying for the pilots, the crew members, guardian angels to guide the plane and anything else that comes to mind for safe journeys.

While sleeping, I hate to be touched because it wakes me up. But when my husband reaches for my hand? I know he is praying. For me. For our son. For life's scary situations. And I always feel a sense of love, strength, and surety emanating from his hands.

But we don't have to have an actual person next to us to "hold their hand" so to speak. Oftentimes when I can't sleep, my thoughts turn to loved ones and friends who need my prayers. So I spiritually hold their hand as I lift them up before the throne of God. It's a lovely way to turn irritating insomnia into a positive prayer session.

Often, when I pray, I ask God to just "take me by the hand and show me what to do." Like a toddler who needs direction, I frequently feel overwhelmed and in need of some kind of guidance. Thankfully, the Bible has many examples of this.

David writes in Psalm 73,

> "When my heart was grieved and my spirit
>   embittered,
> I was senseless and ignorant; I was a brute beast
>   before you.
> Yet I am always with you;
>   *You hold me by my right hand.*

You guide me with your counsel,
   And afterward you will take me into glory.
Whom have I in heaven but you?
   And earth has nothing I desire besides you.
My flesh and my heart may fail, but God is the
   strength of my heart
And my portion forever." (verses 21-26,
   emphasis mine).

꙾ꞏ꙾

*God isn't repelled by our craving need of rescue
from our fears—it compels Him
to comfort and draw near.*

꙾ꞏ꙾

"For I am the Lord your God who *takes hold of
   your right hand* and says to you,
Do not fear; I will help you" (Isaiah 41:13
   emphasis mine).

Unlike what we see in the media during histrionic healing services, Jesus didn't need to smack someone on the
forehead and compel them to fall backward for healing. He
often just held their hands.

When Jairus, the distraught synagogue leader's daugh-
ter died, Jesus didn't blow in her face, shout, or push her on
the forehead. He gently and calmly took her by the hand.

"They laughed at him, knowing that she was dead. But
he took her by the hand and said, 'My child, get up!' Her
spirit returned, and at once she stood up. Then Jesus told
them to give her something to eat" (Luke 8:53-54).

With His hands, Jesus touched people, healed them, ate

with them, and rescued them. When Simon Peter's faith wavered in the waves, Jesus didn't wag a finger at him. He didn't throw up his hands in despair. He reached down and grasped his hand.

Jesus lets us know we can rely on his sure grip. When confronted and challenged by his fellow Jewish leaders regarding his divinity, He replied,

> "My sheep listen to my voice; I know them, and they follow me. I give them eternal life, and they shall never perish; *no one will snatch them out of my hand.* My Father, who has given them to me, is greater than all; *no one can snatch them out of my Father's hand.* I and the Father are one." (John 10: 27-30 emphasis mine).

There are strong currents of fear, despair, and worry in our world. Often, we feel tossed about by the waves of circumstances beyond our control. But there is a hand we can hold—the One who stills the waters stills our fears, and still touches our lives with His reassuring grasp. If sea otters can do it, so can we. Reach out and hold His hand.

Moonlit Musings

1. Do you have any sweet memories of holding someone's hand? A grandparent? A friend? How did that make you feel?
2. Is there someone's hand you like to hold? Someone who's touch makes you feel safe?
3. Who in your life might need your hand to reach out to them—either literally or figuratively in prayer?
4. Which of the verses about God the Father or Jesus holding our hands spoke the most comfort to you?

Prayer

Heavenly Father,

What a wonderful world you have made! The charming sea otters and other creatures of night are all a part of your beautiful creation. Thank you for promising me that no one or nothing can snatch me from your hand. I need to hold your hand more and more these days. This world sometimes feels out of control, as if it's tilting off its axis. But you have promised that you will always be with me. Like the apostle Peter sinking below the waves, please help me to remember I can always reach out and hold your hand. Thank you for always being there.

In Jesus' name, amen.

CHAPTER 2

Bat

As a nature enthusiast, I'm supposed to like bats. But I don't. They make my skin crawl. This is due to a long history of encounters with them, and none of them are good.

I understand their role in the cycle of life, and that they are also nighttime pollinators, but I feel the same revulsion toward them that others do for spiders or snakes. *Shudder.*

Madison, Wisconsin, is a city on an isthmus. Which is a long, skinny peninsula-like land bridge with large lakes on either side. Lake Mendota is on the west, and Lake Monona is on the east. Granted, these are nowhere near the size of the two immense Great Lakes that border this state: Lake Superior and Lake Michigan, but they are larger than average and host lots and lots of insects. And insects are what bats like to eat.

Growing up across the street from Lake Mendota, our old home had frequent bat visitors. They found some crevice to squeeze into and would flap around our house—particularly in the fall and in the evenings. We developed a routine to deal with this. My older siblings and I would slam shut our bedroom doors while my mother—a Grace Kelly lookalike and tennis aficionado—would grab her racket and volley the bat against the wall. In bat vs. Mom, she always won. Then, she would deposit it in the trash.

This didn't always quell them. Some mornings, I would walk through our garage on my way to school and hear last night's bat rustling and squeaking in the garbage. *Shudder.*

One night, my brother was asleep and reached up to scratch his thick hair. His hand closed around a furry, squirming creature. Now wide awake and heart pounding, he launched it against his bedroom wall with all the strength a 15-year-old with a pretty solid arm could. But he confessed, "My heart didn't quiet down for hours—it was a little tough to get back to sleep." *Shudder.*

Years later when his new wife installed a bat house in their garden, I gave him an incredulous side-eye and muttered, "You must *really* love her."

When I rented an apartment with my sorority sister one summer, a bat got trapped inside the wall of our room and spent the night squeaking and fluttering against the wall. Then, of course, he escaped and dive-bombed our heads, which were under our sheets, while we screamed like 6-year-olds. *Shudder.*

All that is to say, there's a reason I behaved the way I did while on a date in Sydney, Australia.

My date and I just had a lovely dinner near the Sydney

Harbor bridge. I didn't know him very well, but he was nice enough and had good manners. It was a warm evening, and we were strolling along the water admiring the lights twinkling across the harbor. My date leaned his head back while we walked under a particularly massive, spreading, Moreton Bay fig tree and marveled, "Wow! Look at all those fruit bats above us!" *Shudder.*

Fruit bats? I knew that they were much, much bigger than my midwestern bats. In fact, a fruit bat's wingspan is over a yard wide. And while some people refer to these huge bats as "flying foxes," I am not fooled. They are bats, some of the biggest in the world. My eyes got wide, my breath hitched in my throat, and I did what any 6-foot-tall girl would do who was terrified of a bat swooping down on her: I immediately dropped to all fours on the pavement in my cute little sundress and began scuttling like a drunken crab to get out from under the tree.

My date stood rooted, slack-jawed, and gobsmacked. *"What's wrong with you?"* he asked. This was quite a departure from my acceptable dinner manners.

I couldn't answer him at first. I was too busy concentrating on staying low to the ground and scooting out from under that tree. I grunted and gasped in my ungainly progression, utterly oblivious to what others nearby might think of me.

"Bats!" I replied matter-of-factly once I got out from under the spreading branches and could stand up. I calmly flicked pieces of pavement out of the palms of my hands and straightened my dress. "I. Can't. Stand. Them." (I didn't explain that I didn't want to be the first target if they decided to swoop or poo). We never went out again.

While I obviously have my issues with bats, I'm not ignorant of the beneficial services they provide.

For one thing that's dear to my heart, they eat mosquitoes. Lots and lots of mosquitoes—up to 1,200 an hour. They often eat their body weight in insects every night, which helps keep bug populations controlled. There is one bat in the southwest—the pallid bat—which can eat the most venomous scorpion in North America, the Arizona bark scorpion, which is fatal to humans. So, there's that.

Along with gobbling up all the nasties, bats provide a vital service to our ecosystem by pollinating and dispersing plants at night. Not all plants bloom in the day; some do so only at night, and that's another place where bats contribute.

There are over 1,100 species of bats in the world and 40 species in the United States. The most common ones that I probably encountered (I assure you, I did not capture or examine them!) are the little brown bats—about 2 inches long—with a wingspan of up to 11 inches, and the big brown bats—not much bigger—almost 3 inches in body length. And bats are the only flying mammals. You might think, what about flying squirrels? They don't fly; they simply glide.

Bats are long-lived and slow to produce. They usually have only one pup a year, so when their numbers are threatened by pesticides, wind turbines, habitat loss, Mom's tennis racket, or weather, it can have devastating effects on the population. They are, however, pretty amazingly resilient to weather. They hibernate over winter and in the summer they can withstand temperature changes of nearly 120 degrees Fahrenheit.

Bat

What's probably best known about bats is their ability to navigate in the dark. It's a myth that all bats are blind. But their vision is secondary to their proficiency in echolocation. Bats emit a high-frequency sound similar to ships using sonar. This sound bounces off objects, which then tells them the location and size of prey by listening to the sound echo that returns to them. Through echolocation, they can navigate where they are, in relation to prey or objects. While this is admirable in bats, it's foolish when we try to do it.

Many of us use a sort of echolocation in our daily lives to determine how we are doing. (I know this because I have a black belt in this practice, and a few of my friends admit they do it, too.) We note what others are wearing, achieving, buying, and doing and then measure where we stand in relation to that. I feel better about myself if my "echolocation" tells me I'm not the biggest girl in the room. I feel a little worse about myself if my self-importance sonar indicates I'm not the most successful person in a group. (How on earth do you definitively measure "success" anyway?) And I notice men do this, too. They stand a little straighter when they see that other men nearby are taller. We unconsciously echolocate our position or success in life based on where others are. Unlike bats, we don't need to.

One of the early verses I memorized from the Bible was Psalms 119:105, "Your word is a lamp for my feet, a light on my path." For me, this meant that if you want to know where you stand in life, it's in God's Word. If you want a light for your future path, to see where you're headed, it's in God's Word. How does this work?

When I feel less than others, thanks to my faulty echolocation, I re-locate with a reminder. While I've often felt Psalm 23 was for grandmas or those going down with a sinking ship, I've come to appreciate it more as I walk through life. It has excellent reminders of where we stand, Who stands with us, and what our future holds.

> "The Lord is my shepherd,
>   I lack nothing.
> He lets me rest in grassy meadows;
>   he leads me to restful waters; he keeps me alive.
> He guides me in proper paths for the sake of his
>   good name.
> Even when I walk through the darkest valley,
>   I fear no danger because you are with me.
> Your rod and your staff—they protect me.
> You set a table for me right in front of
>   my enemies.
> You bathe my head in oil;
>   My cup is so full it spills over!
> Yes, goodness and faithful love will pursue me all
>   the days of my life,
> And I will live in the Lord's house as long as I
>   live" (CEB version).

God's Word tells us we were planned for, seen by Him, and chosen by Him before the foundation of the world.

> "Long before he laid down earth's foundations, he had us in mind, had settled on us as the focus of his love, to be made whole and holy by his love. Long, long ago he decided to adopt us into his family through Jesus Christ. (What pleasure he took in planning this!) He wanted us to enter into the celebration of his lavish gift-giving by the hand of his beloved Son" (Ephesians 1:4-6 The Message).

We are uniquely and wonderfully made—so there is no need for comparison.

> "For You formed my inward parts;
> You wove me in my mother's womb.
> I will give thanks to You,
> for I am fearfully and wonderfully made (Psalm
> 139:14 NASB).

And our future is secure.

> "For I know the plans I have for you,"
> declares the LORD,
> "plans to prosper you and not to harm you,
> Plans to give you hope and a future" (Jeremiah 29:11).

When I use scripture to reorient my standing in the world, I see the fallacy in using echolocation in regard to others. It's a constantly shifting environment that makes it difficult to gain my footing. When I echolocate on things that mislead, I'm full of comparison and competition. When I get my bearings on what God says about me, it fosters feelings of compassion and service. It helps reorient my outlook from "How do I compare?" to "How do I care?" Without a sure foundation, I'm left with my cauldron stew of insecurities, jealousies, and miseries straight from the pit.

꙳ · ꙳

When we grab hold of what God says about us,
we move from How do I compare?
to How can I care?
It's an outward vs. an inward focus.

꙳ · ꙳

Echolocation is excellent for bats, but it's a faulty and dark way to navigate where we stand in life.

I find it interesting that the common collective noun for a group of bats can be called a colony, but it can also be called a *cauldron* of bats. It figures.

Moonlit Musings

1. Are there any creatures (like snakes, bats, spiders) that you just can't abide?
2. How do you react around them? What is your response based on?
3. Are there any people you find yourself "echolocating" with? (Bouncing your sense of well-being off them based on their achievements?)
4. Which of these verses helps you the most in realizing God's perfect and secure location or position in life for you?
5. What can you do to refocus when you realize you're losing your bearings?

Prayer

Heavenly Father,

This world tells me to navigate my path based on popular culture, media images, or the latest trend. But you tell me your Word is the compass by which I can faithfully determine where I stand and where I'm going. Help me apply Psalm 119:105 to my daily life: "Your word is a lamp for my feet, a light on my path."

In Jesus' name, amen.

CHAPTER 3

Moth

T he night breezes flutter the drapes at our bedroom window. Most evenings, I insist on the window being open, even if it's just a crack due to rain. Partly this is due to my internal temperature being much higher than my husband's, and partly because I just like the cool, fresh air and listening to the lonesome hoot of the owls across the ravine.

Flutter. . .flutter. The drapes whisper against the windowsill. I turn over on my pillow. When I find it difficult to drift off to sleep, I try fixing my mind on what is happening outside in the quiet, dark, and peaceful places. Tonight, I think about something I know is fluttering outside my window under the inky cover of night. I don't see them, but I know they are out there. While my eyelashes flutter in response to REM sleep, furry creatures are busily at work, fluttering amongst the flowers, weeds, and trees.

The white-lined sphinx moth hovers her stout, furry body with pink, brown, and white striped wings above my petunias that spill over the edges of the window boxes. Sometimes, the sphinx moth is called the hawk moth or hummingbird moth because of her unique ability to hover like a hummingbird or a bat. Unlike a butterfly's smooth, clubbed antennae, her furry, comb-like antennae enable her to pick up the aroma of my flowers wafting on the night breezes.

While hovering, she unfurls her long tube-like mouth section called a proboscis. She inserts the tip of the proboscis into the flower and sips up nectar. Then she flutters off to the next.

I drowsily think about one of my favorites, the Ornate Tiger Moth, with its dramatic yellow and black striped markings. I found him a few nights before, resting on the downward-facing, landscape lighting fixture. Despite the light fixture being HOA approved and their good intentions, I don't approve. Because this false moonlight kept him there most of the night instead of off fluttering and pollinating. Landscape lighting does this to many moths. His striking pale yellow and black stripes make him easy to spot but also easy prey the longer he sits there. He was a wonder to behold, with deep orange and black underwings. But it was sad to see him rendered helpless by the lure of the lamplight.

A nondescript, mottled, brown moth lifts off from the side of a tree. While resting there, he thoroughly blended in with the gray tree bark. Once he unfolds his wings, we see a startling jolt of coral, red, or pink on his under-wings. Hence his name, the underwing moth. He lands on a flower, his furry body—much fluffier than the pollinator, superstar bee—nestles into the pollen and reproductive organs of the flower. His extreme shagginess collects more pollen than bees can, and like most moths, his range is wider too.

While bees and butterflies get all the attention and photo shoots, our quiet, unsung hero and nondescript moth does more work. Bees have distinct ranges that keep them closer to the nest, while moths have a far greater range. Moths pollinate the same things the bees and butterflies do, but they also visit plants that the other pollinators miss during the day. Like night-blooming flowers whose perfume exudes only in the evenings, such as Datura, Night-blooming Jasmine, Brugmansia, and Moonflowers. They also pollinate blossoms with harder-to-reach nectar like Nicotiana (flowering tobacco), Gardenia, and Morning glories. So essentially, these unassuming, drab pollinators are doing more work than their flashier, fluttering relatives who get most of the attention and adoration.

I used to think of moths in negative terms—they were a pest in the pantry. They caused me to worry about wool sweaters. They were sort of creepy in some way. With their gray, black, and brown coloring, they weren't lovely and attention-grabbing like a swallowtail butterfly or the stained-glass majesty of the Monarch. It's easy to overlook moths. They are designed to blend in with tree bark, wood, pebbles, and fallen leaves. They blend in, hoping not to be noticed until the covering veil of dusk descends. Then, they unfurl their camouflage and get to work.

At a glance, one way to tell whether you are looking at a moth versus a butterfly at twilight or dawn is to look at their antennae. A butterfly's antennae are slender and smooth with a club—a thickened dot—at the end. A moth's antennae are furry and comb-like. They use these to pick up scents wafting on evening breezes.

I didn't give them a second thought until I started walking our dog late at night. Just before bed, around 10 or 11 p.m., I head out for what we call a "door walk." This means it's not around the block; it's just right by the front door, so he empties his bladder. But because we live in an area with mountain lions and coyotes, I have a flashlight. As I focused my light down into the ravine and creek, the beam caught the dance of the magical moths. I started noticing their colorations and behaviors and thinking about their prolific pollination while most people and creatures of the world are asleep.

We are, metaphorically, asleep to much of the world's beauty. Whether it's because the media lens is focused on the brash and bold, or because we are so caught up in our own worries that we haven't learned to slow down and train our eyes to see. But there is so much fluttering right by us in our peripheral vision that is far lovelier, if we just stop and look.

I was reminded of this a while ago when I stumbled upon Darlene.

It was a brilliant fall day, with crisp air and a perfect cobalt sky. I was planning to go on a bike ride after I completed my errand. With an armload of books that needed to be dropped off at church, I breezed into the upstairs room to stash them. But I heard a strange sound.

I turned around; the room appeared to be empty. But then she straightened up from behind a half wall and nearly made me scream.

"Hi there!" she said with a huge grin and a dustpan in her hand. Her hair was a bird's nest tangle, and she looked absolutely thrilled. Although she wasn't much over five foot two and appeared to be in her seventies, she gave my six-foot frame a startle.

"What are you doing?" I asked.

"Cleaning!" she said like it was a privilege. Many thoughts went through my mind. *Didn't churches hire that out for a cleaning service? Was she alone with this big job? Didn't she have any helpers? Wasn't she too old for this?*

"Do you do this often?" I asked. (Maybe she was just filling in.)

"Yep! I do this every Tuesday. It's my love offering." She shrugged her shoulders and bent down to get the last crumbs of what had escaped her earlier.

I stood there slack-jawed. Her happy devotion to this unsung, menial task gave me pause.

It was clear to me in that instant that I *never* chose to serve in ways that went completely unnoticed and under the radar. I like words of approval. I like being noticed. I want to be congratulated on doing something well. The limelight draws me like a moth.

But thanks to Darlene, when the congregation gathered in the foyer to have coffee and greet each other, when the helpers rocked babies in the nursery, and when the youth met upstairs in the overflow room, it was all because of her they could do so in a clean and tidy environment. Her unheralded service in the background paved the way for others to shine.

I felt like slithering out of there, ashamed of my "perform for applause" tendencies while standing in the presence of someone who was clearly experiencing the simple joy of service.

"Beautiful," I said to myself, lost in thoughts of self-loathing.

"Yes, it is a beautiful day, isn't it?" she replied. But I wasn't talking about the weather.

You don't have to be in church to discover and be awed by the beautiful, hidden service of others. In fact, often it's too distracting with the shoulds, oughts, and noise that church politics can create. But if you look around and take time to notice, there are hidden figures and unsung heroes quietly laboring away all around us.

Unfortunately, the world applauds the loud, lascivious, and loutish as opposed to the heroic, quiet service that millions perform daily. It's almost as if it wasn't filmed and posted somewhere, it wasn't worthy of notice. Nothing could be further from the truth.

Jesus talked about performing—or serving to be seen—in the book of Matthew. "Be careful not to practice your righteousness in front of others to be seen by them. If you do, you will have no reward from your Father in heaven" (Matthew 6:1).

But our society and our egos battle against this. I used to joke with my husband (because often it was sadly true), "What's the use of being good if only you and God know it?" Meaning, I want to do the right thing, but darn it, it would be nice to be applauded for it.

I believe the truly heroic and selfless and most Christ-like among us don't have these struggles or thoughts. They see a need and step up, whether or not there are cameras or clapping. And usually, the most beautiful moments are when the help is hidden and unheralded.

Teresa Hsu was known as "Singapore's Mother Teresa" for her lifelong devotion to helping the aged, sick, and destitute locally. She started several charities and spent all her money on acquiring housing and help for the aged and sick who had nowhere else to turn. Often serving people decades younger than herself, at 110 (she died at 113), she was still running around and serving where she could. While most of the world applauded Mother Teresa in India, Teresa Hsu served more people and longer, mostly out of the limelight.

We don't have to start up charities or serve until we are 110 years old to be of service or accomplish something valuable. While I'll never be the first to help someone move, I don't mind giving rides to the airport. I may feel disgruntled if I'm the only one emptying the dishwasher 3 days in a row (does everyone else have broken arms? I think to myself), it is an act of service to do it graciously and without complaint. Sometimes, it's the little things that are so greatly appreciated.

My friend Serena lives in a town where, despite starting up walking groups and attending a church, it's been hard to find friends to rely on. When she needed a ride home from a medical procedure, she was deeply grateful to the person who helped and gave her a safe ride home.

Like the Pharisees and guests at dinner, we tend to wrinkle our noses when something akin to "washing the feet" of others is presented to us. We think perhaps maybe someone less educated could do that menial work? Giving rides, sacrificing our time and offering help without recognition doesn't jibe with our coffee-cup motto of, "Be awesome today!"

My husband is a big fan of books by Robert Coles. We have at least ten of his books. Most of them are about the necessity and joys of service. Because this Pulitzer Prize-winning professor emeritus from Harvard knows the secret about service: those that serve others instead of themselves find the most joy and satisfaction in life. While the culture around us screams that we should be "awesome!" or at least be noticed for something if we want to feel significant and liked. But the data says otherwise. To serve unnoticed, without applause or likes, is the secret to joy, purpose in life, and contentment.

This isn't a new concept. Before Jesus taught the disciples how to pray using the outline of the "Our Father" prayer, He talked about serving and giving in secret. So apparently, it was right up there in importance with that prayer.

> "So when you give to the needy, do not announce it with trumpets, as the hypocrites do in the synagogues and on the streets, to be honored by others. Truly I tell you, they have received their reward in full. But when you give to the needy, do not let your left hand know what your right hand is doing, so that your giving may be in secret. Then your Father, who sees what is done in secret, will reward you" (Matthew 6:2-4).

Joy and satisfaction in life is not found in
being noticed and applauded,
but serving others in secret
for which God said will be lauded.

When we serve in secret, shun the spotlight, and don't get recognition for our undercover works, whether big or small, we are like moths—pollinating the world with the poetic presence of love. We can rest assured that Someone *does* notice. He is applauding, and His reward is sure.

Moonlit Musings

1. Who do you know who performs service for others that the world isn't applauding?
2. When have you served others without recognition? How did you feel about that?
3. Are you familiar with any moths in your area? Try these websites to see beautiful moths.

https://www.treehugger.com/moth-species-more-beautiful-than-butterflies-4864257
https://www.birdsandblooms.com/gardening/garden-bugs/moth-pictures/

4. Is there anyone you could call attention to, or thank personally, for their unsung service to others? This could be as simple as a smiling doorman, a cheerful bagger at the grocery store, or a school crossing guard.

Prayer

Heavenly Father,

Thank you for sending Jesus as an example of how we can serve others. Although the world tells me it's more important to be noticed and applauded, you value humble service. Call to my attention others who are serving unnoticed, that I might encourage them. Show me areas where I could serve someone at home, or in my community, without fanfare but as a love offering to you. Thank you for your assurance that, "whatever you did for one of the least of these brothers and sisters of mine, you did for me" (Matthew 25:40).

In Jesus' name, amen.

CHAPTER 4

Coyote

The alluring, fluffy object kept twitching. Back and forth, it swayed, golden and rust amongst the reeds next to the pond, beckoning in the dusk of the waning day. The young duckling left his family and swam closer. What was this? So interesting! Twitch. . .twitch, the strange plant seemed to call to the innocent paddler— until a warning honk from its mother caused him to pause. Maybe this wasn't safe? The straggling duckling looked back at his family across the pond. At that moment, the water and reeds exploded with fur, teeth, water, flapping, and quacking.

This was no plant moving in the wind! It was a coyote's tail, and now the dog had turned, lunging and snapping at the young duckling. Fortunately, our young duck escaped the ruse of the coyote, but many are not so fortunate.

Coyotes are notorious for their clever, conniving, and slinky ways. While we've managed to eradicate the wolf so thoroughly that after 100 years, they had to be reintroduced to Yellowstone National Park, coyotes thrive no matter how hard people have tried to get rid of them.

A native of arid areas, the coyote has learned to adapt to major cities, forests, seashores, and every part of the United States. But its behavior is the same. Wily, cunning, clever, and scary-smart, it can put domestic dogs to shame.

Our family has long been enthusiasts of dogs in general, but German shepherds in particular. My parents, my brother, and my sister have all had them. We love them because they are one of the most intelligent breeds, loyal, obedient, and just a joy to have around. Police and military units depend on them for their intelligence and ability to learn tasks. But I have to admit, they are not a match for determined and crafty coyotes.

Author James Cornett has written over 20 books on desert subjects, and coyotes are his specialty. He once watched a pair of coyotes approach an off-leash German shepherd as if to play. They crouched low, wagged their tails, and ran about, and the shepherd joined in on the fun. But although he was much bigger and stronger, this shepherd soon tired. And after they had lured him little by little out into the desert, they quickly disposed of him. He was later found in a ditch, half-eaten.

I had heard of this luring behavior from people living in wooded areas near me. They claimed that a coyote will pretend to be injured and whimper in the bushes. When a domestic dog goes to investigate, he is ambushed by a pack of coyotes.

Online, there are many accounts of ranchers and country folk having witnessed this. They write:

> "Saw this happen to a new neighbor who insisted they were friendly with her Pomeranian. She thought we were terrible for suggesting she shoot the coyote that would look through her back slider. After the inevitable happened and she helplessly watched the coyote lope off over the horizon with her dog in its mouth, she wants us to shoot them all.
>
> Coyotes will often lure a dog out so the pack can get them. Often it will be a bitch in heat. We rolled a stump in one area that had a den and pulled out 56 dog and cat collars. They had been collecting the local ones for many years.
>
> Do not mess around with coyotes. They will kill any domestic animals you have and they're smart. So you need to make sure any animals you have are safe from coyotes. I know people who've been out walking their tiny dogs to have them snatched up by a coyote or let them out in the backyard to go to the bathroom only to get jumped and killed by a coyote."

It didn't seem to matter the size or strength of the domestic dog, either. One man talked about his massive Malamute/Boxer mixed dog (80 pounds) and his Mastiff/Pit Bull/ Husky dog (90 pounds)—extremely strong, large, and intimidating—but they were no match for the wily coyote.

Coyotes don't just lure domestic dogs; they know how to lure food from gullible humans. James Cornett witnessed a coyote repeatedly crossing a busy road in Death Valley with a limp. Park visitors would stop, photograph the animal, and then offer food to the "poor, injured animal." But when the cars left, so did the limp. Cornett would try to get closer to the crafty canine to get photos of this, but the coyote would run off at full tilt—and with absolutely no limp. The animal had learned that limping in front of tourists would get him food. Clever!

They are also smart enough to get other animals to work with them. Coyotes have been observed working with badgers to capture food. The coyote will run the animal down, and when the tired prey burrows into its den—or jumps down the rabbit hole—the badger digs in after it.

Coyotes in the wilderness eat rodents, rabbits, and other small prey. Ranchers know they will attack sheep as well. But as they have adapted to city living, their meals consist of trash and small domestic pets. When I see notices of missing pets in our semi-rural area, I often think, "They are not missing; they've been eaten." But of course, I keep these thoughts to myself; I know the distress of a missing pet.

The best way to keep them from threatening your furry friends is to keep your pets indoors or on a tight leash at night. Keep pet food inside and garbage locked down. And forget free-range chickens; that's just a smorgasbord to a coyote. But they are so cunning that fences must be 7 feet high and sunk deep into the ground because they will climb over and dig under your best efforts.

The first time I heard coyotes at night, I was confused. The yips, yelps, and howls sounded so high-pitched and mewling that I thought it was a band of feral cats. But my husband assured me, "Not cats. Not wolves. Coyotes." Although they are mainly nocturnal, I have seen them boldly loping through a field at midday, not perturbed at all by my presence.

At a distance, it can be hard to tell whether you are looking at a coyote, German shepherd, or wolf. Coyotes look a lot like German shepherds from a distance. But they are usually much leaner, long-legged, with a pointer snout and bigger ears. The coyote's fur is a grizzled gray, and their bushy tail has a black tip. When dogs run, their tails are usually up. Wolves run with their tails held straight behind them, and coyotes run with their tails down. And if it's nighttime, you won't hear the lonesome, deep howl of a wolf. The coyote's vocalization will be much higher pitched yip-yips and almost meow-mewling-howling. But I hope never to encounter one at night while walking my dog. Our little white Bichon thinks he's Goliath; but of course, he would just be a marshmallow appetizer for Wily E. Coyote, so I'm very wary at night.

I think the crafty wiles of the coyote have infected the American church as well. While I understand the pastors desire to grow and influence their communities, I am wary and somewhat repelled to see pastors and church boards wholeheartedly adopting the shrewd attitude of the coyote.

Sometimes, this is so prevalent and accepted that we don't even notice or flinch when they implement these methods. Also, we are so enmeshed with the world's ways that we think it makes sense to act just as wily, crafty, and cunning.

My husband's father was a gentle-hearted pastor who fully trusted God and refused to resort to the ways of the world to accomplish things. When he had a radio program, he was urged to ask for support—for people to send money to fund the ministry. We shrug our shoulders at this and think, "Just common business sense." But not to him. It appalled him to seek money from the public instead of from God. Like George Müller, who started orphanages and ran a massive program housing the street children of Bristol, England, he never asked for money. He relied on God to meet his needs. And God did.

This sounds quaint to us in the 21st century, but it still works this way in heavenly realms. We don't have to adopt the crafty and wily ways of the world to accomplish our ends.

In his book *Fresh Wind, Fresh Fire*, pastor Jim Cymbala recounts that when he started his small, wobbly little church in Brooklyn, prayer was all they had. Prayer brought in everything: people, more pray-ers, and money. It was all built with prayer, not impassioned pleas for financial support or Wall Street methods of raising capital.

Today, we see churches adopting the ways of the world to grow, add to their numbers, and become a force in society. Thus, churches hire management consultants, attendance numbers are discretely taken, and other methods and means of growth are utilized in a Machiavellian attitude of "the ends justify the means."

When a friend asked his pastor if the church board might not gather to pray for financial needs *first* instead of emailing the flock for more money, he was met with the pastor's retort, "How much prayer is enough?" Seeing such a brazen, cynical view of relying on God took my friend's breath away. But this is not rare, it's everywhere.

Either Jesus is who He says He is, or He's lying. In one of His weakest physical moments, when He was most likely to fall prey to the world's ways, Satan taunted Him after 40 days of fasting with, "If you are the Son of God, tell these stones to become bread." Jesus answered, "It is written: 'Man shall not live on bread alone, but on every word that comes from the mouth of God' "(Matthew 4:3-4).

Jesus quoted Deuteronomy 8:3 when God spoke to the Israelites about the importance of their dependence on God.

> "Remember how the LORD your God led you all the way in the wilderness these forty years, to humble and test you in order to know what was in your heart, whether or not you would keep His commands. He humbled you, causing you to hunger and then feeding you with manna, which neither you nor your ancestors had known, to teach you that man does not live on bread alone but on every word that comes from the mouth of the LORD" (Deuteronomy 8:2-4).

The stress here is not so much stones vs. bread and assuaging hunger, but more about relying on God to deliver. Whether that's food, finances, or furnishings, He is able. He is our source. He is serious about our reliance on Him in ancient times and now. We don't have to mimic the wily ways of the world to manipulate or strong-arm our deliverance.

When David disobeyed God and counted the numbers of his people (relying on himself and strength in numbers instead of God), he was punished. When Moses decided to be theatrical and strike the rock for water instead of speaking to it like God told him to, he suffered the consequences of never seeing the promised land that for years he had labored. I wonder what glorious outcomes we are forfeiting when we rely on the world's manipulations and machinations to achieve our ends instead of relying on God?

✦

When we rely on the world's ways and conniving, we miss out on the miraculous gifts of God providing.

✦

I wrote this verse in the front of the first Bible I bought myself, because I knew it was the perfect antidote for how I usually approached life.

> "Trust in the LORD with all your heart
> And do not lean on your own understanding.
> In all your ways acknowledge Him,
> And He will make your paths straight.
> Do not be wise in your own eyes;
> Fear the LORD and turn away from evil.
> It will be healing to your body
> And refreshment to your bones"
> (Proverbs 3:5-7 NASB).

We all have a choice in our daily lives and decisions to make. Will I be a cunning coyote and approach things with the world's ways—because the ends justify the means? Or will I lay down my own understanding and be a disciple of Christ?

I saw something yesterday that illustrated this point perfectly. The man ahead of me was walking his dog and wearing a black Tshirt. In white letters across the back it said, "Not my way, YAHWEH."

ෂ෨ · ෨ෂ

We all have a choice to make,
My will be done? Or Thy will be done?

ෂ෨ · ෨ෂ

The spirit of a coyote says, "I will do what it takes to get what I want. *My will* be done." And it lures us off track with promises, but ultimately destroys the glittering future we could have had.

The spirit of Christ says, "I choose to lean not on my own understanding. *Thy will* be done." And we walk into a life free from tricky manipulations and conniving. Even the strongest dogs are no match for that wily coyote. Trot after our Good Shepherd; He has promised us guidance and green pastures to inhabit.

Moonlit Musings

1. In what ways have you adopted the coyote's cunning to get what you want instead of praying and asking God first?
2. Have you seen evidence of this in your church as well? (Pray for your pastor.)
3. Why do you think many believers don't believe God will provide for them the way He did with Jim Cymbala and George Müller?
4. In what areas or decisions in your life could you apply the Proverbs 3:5-7 verses?

Prayer

Heavenly Father,

Thank you that your resources are limitless. Thank you that time and again in the Bible you show me you can and will provide. This world offers me so much at a moment's notice that I struggle to wait to see what you think or how you want to provide for me. Please give me patience for your timing and help me to stop my knee-jerk, "My will be done," and exchange it for "Thy will be done." Then I can say like Psalm 118:23, "The LORD has done this, and it is marvelous in our eyes."

In Jesus' name, amen.

CHAPTER 5

Badger

J ames Herriot watched the tall young man with a black
   walrus mustache and dark eyes step down from the
train. By his side was a big lurcher dog (a cross between a
greyhound and a coonhound). His battered suitcase indi-
cated he needed the veterinary job he was being offered,
but that's not what distracted the British author. Draped
over the traveler's left shoulder was a large, hairy animal.
Worn somewhat in the style of a mink stole or cardigan.
But this was grey, large, and heavy.

He put out his hand and grinned. "Mr. Herriot?"

"Yes…yes…" I shook his hand. "You'll be Calum
Buchanan."

"That's right."

"Good, good…but what's that on your shoulder?"

"That's Marilyn."

"Marilyn?"

"Yes, my badger."[1]

Calum explains to the surprised James Herriot that his pet badger goes everywhere with him. And he wasn't kidding. Calum brought Marilyn draped across his shoulders to vet visits on farms, inside the Herriot's home, and nearly caused a riot at the taciturn local pub. Marilyn didn't mind being slung about his shoulders, pet by children, or living the odd life of a vet's companion. If you know much about badgers, this is extraordinary.

Badgers are renowned for their aggression, tenacity, and tendency to do poorly in captivity. (Maybe this is why my alma mater, the University of Wisconsin, chose the badger as its mascot.) Badgers can grow up to 20 to 34 inches long from head to tail, and weigh between 9 and 39 pounds. Their bodies are flat and wedge-shaped, with coarse hair that can be black, brown, or grey. The feet are broad with long claws. Found throughout most of North America, they are members of the Mustelidae family, which includes ferrets, minks, otters, weasels, and wolverines.

Although they have a cute face with black and white stripes, don't be deceived. God built the badger ready for a fight. They have dense, thick fur and muscular necks to help them fight off enemies. When faced with a predator, badgers will vocalize with growling and hissing. If that doesn't deter the intruder, they can emit a musky odor, much like a skunk. While the smell is not as intense or unpleasant as a skunk's, it's definitely a deterrent. Threats from wolves or mountain lions don't faze the badger. His thick fur and loose skin allow him to twist around after being grabbed from behind to sink his canines into his attacker. But usually, he will just dig backward and disappear underground within seconds. Once they have dug deep into a den and clamped down on their prey—like a prairie dog—their unique jaw structure helps them win most of the time.

Their jaw sits in their skull with a special notch that locks the upper mandible into place. This means it's impossible to dislocate an American badger's jaw. So when his prey is stuck deep in a burrow underground, the badger's powerful neck and clamped jaw usually wrenches them out of their hiding place. (And it explains why our clever coyote teams up with him after running down prey—see the Coyote chapter.)

Badgers are omnivores and will eat meat they've caught such as gophers, as well as carrion left behind like roadkill. This way they become an essential member of the environmental clean-up crew.

At first glance, they don't seem all that dangerous because their favorite pastime is sleeping. As nocturnal predators, they sleep all day in their snug dens, which can be hundreds of feet long. And in deep winter, they can sleep for weeks. When they enter this deep sleep, it is called a torpor. His heartbeat slows down, much like a hibernating bear. But badgers don't enter into full hibernation like bears do. There's a reason this lumbering, furry guy on stout legs has cozy dens that are so long and extensive. His formidable digging feet.

The badger is one of the world's fastest and strongest

digging animals. They've even been seen digging through parking lot asphalt and getting underground within two minutes. Faster than two people with shovels, their flat bodies and powerful legs help them reach gophers in their burrows and dig their extensive underground homes. Their front feet, propelled by their sturdy shoulders, are partially webbed with claws that don't retract and are up to two inches long. Their back feet are slightly smaller and made to shove away the soil the front legs dig out. When it comes to digging, this guy doesn't play around.

One account of the badger's extraordinary digging capabilities was caught on camera in Utah. The calf of a cow had died, and the badger discovered it. With immense confidence and enthusiasm, he set about digging a temporary grave for the carcass so he could feast upon it for days to come. Over the course of four days, he furiously dug, and the dirt flew. He succeeded. Despite the calf weighing 50 pounds to the badger's 16, our digger was undaunted. He was able to feast on the calf for many days, thanks to his diligent work.

I admire that kind of confidence and enthusiasm over a monumental task. Instead of considering such an enormous undertaking as far too difficult, the badger knew he was made to dig. The job would get done if he just stuck to what he knew. It reminds me of the fable of two boys. Both wanted a pony for their birthday. But what they were presented with was a horse stall and a pile of manure. One boy sat down and cried. What a raw deal! The other got to work with a shovel, confident that, "There's gotta be a pony under all this!"

People who see the mountain and immediately start

estimating what sort of shovel they'll need to move it inspire me. They see most challenges as simply that, a challenge that will only require some planning and some effort.

If someone needs an event planned with parking issues, menu decisions, children's entertainment, and organizing volunteers, I look like a deer in the headlights of an oncoming car. I blink. I freeze. I think, "Wow, that's a huge undertaking! So many moving parts. I wouldn't know where to start." But I have friends who are the opposite. They roll up their sleeves, a smirk of pleasure tugs at the corners of their mouths, and they can't wait to dive in. What do they know that I don't know?

I could explain it away with, "That's just their gifting—it comes naturally to them." And in part, that's true. But I've come to understand that maybe it's more about attitude, expectations, and belief.

Many of the opportunities we encounter are overlooked or avoided because we don't want to get a shovel. We think it's much too hard. The job's too big. We have no idea where to start.

When my husband was fresh out of university with a PhD in physics, he was unsuccessful in trying to get a teaching job. Nobody needed a physics teacher. Then, a university asked, "We've already filled that position. But maybe you could teach physics part-time as well as computer science?" Well, he had *used* computers. Did he have a degree in computer science? No. But the cool thing about physicists is they know everything is 'figureoutable.' He figured he could learn enough to stay one lesson ahead of the class. And he did. Today, he is a pioneer and leader in Artificial Intelligence. You never know where you'll end up if you just take the first step and say, "Yes!"

When I was asked to teach a history class at our homeschool co-op, I felt overwhelmed. Me? Keep a class of 9 preteen boys occupied? Gulp. Give the shovel to someone else, please. But then I remembered I had been a swim coach many years earlier. I had a son. Surely, I could figure out how to keep them motivated and engaged. What was the worst that could happen? They'd all spit on me and my son would be mortified? Doubtful. It turned out to be more fun than I imagined. Boys need to *move* and love competition, so I engaged them with games, races, and team efforts. We spent a lot of class time laughing. The parents told me it was their boy's favorite class. But if you had told me a year earlier I would be doing that? I would have broken out in a sweat. I would have said, "Teaching? I have no idea how to do that."

We think we need skills, gifts, and talents to overcome the mighty obstacles in our path. Not true. With God, your inability is the perfect opportunity to experience His capability.

The Bible is full of stories of people facing tremendous odds and having no idea how to accomplish the task. Moses was slow of tongue (perhaps a stutterer?) and did not want to be a leader. God used him to confront Pharaoh and set the Israelites free from Egypt. David, the smallest in his family and merely a shepherd of sheep, slayed a giant and became king over Israel. Rahab was a prostitute who hid spies for God and helped them overthrow Jericho. She is listed in Jesus' genealogy.

My husband has a wonderful memory of standing next to the famous missionary and linguistic pioneer Cameron Townsend, singing a hymn. Cameron realized that the indigenous people of Central America needed to read about God in their language. But first, they needed to learn how to read. They needed better health care. They needed work opportunities. So, Cameron got busy. He had the buildings built that needed to be built. He started a health care clinic. He founded and started three organizations: Wycliffe Bible Translators, The Summer Institute of Linguistics, and Jungle Aviation and Radio Service (JAARS). Tom recounts the words that boomed out of Cameron as they stood side by side singing these words:

> Faith mighty faith, the promise sees
> And looks to that alone;
> Laughs at impossibilities
> And cries: It shall be done!

The apostle Paul was no stranger to big jobs, disappointments, and impossibilities. He wanted to be a witness to his people, the Jews. Paul certainly was qualified for that job. He was a Jewish scholar who studied under the famous rabbi Gamaliel. He was such a zealot for God that he was running around killing Christians whom he believed were in gross error. While on his way to Damascus to kill more Christians, Jesus confronted him, and he became a follower. Of course, he would now educate his own people, right? Nope. God sent him to the Gentiles, the non-Jewish people who knew nothing of this God nor His Son, who claimed to be equal to God.

In this assignment to reach the Gentiles, he recounts in his letter to the Corinthians what his new life entailed: imprisonments, beatings, near-death experiences, whipped with 39 lashes (five different times), beaten with rods (three different times), pummeled with stones, shipwrecked (three times), adrift at sea, frequent journeys on foot, and many more dangers. Now that's a momentous challenge!

But this is what he says about accomplishing big jobs:

> "I know what it is to be in need, and I know what it is to have plenty. I have learned the secret of being content in any and every situation, whether well fed or hungry, whether living in plenty or in want. *I can do all this through him who gives me strength*" (Philippians 4:12-13, emphasis the author's).

Paul's secret was relying on God to work through him and not relying on his own strength. We think our talents and business acumen qualify us for big jobs. God is usually just looking for people who are available and willing to work with Him.

❧•◈

> *God cares more about your availability*
> *than your infallibility.*

◈•❧

Jesus explained this concept to His disciples using a vineyard. The fruit doesn't strive, twist, and turn to grow well, it just stays connected to the vine, which has roots deep in the soil. The same principle applies to us.

> "Remain in me, as I also remain in you. No branch can bear fruit by itself; it must remain in the vine. Neither can you bear fruit unless you remain in me. I am the vine; you are the branches. If you remain in me and I in you, you will bear much fruit; apart from me you can do nothing" (John 15:4-5).

If you're like me your mind immediately thinks, "Well, I can do many things without relying on Jesus." Yes, we can. We can pick up our shoes, bake a cake, coach a team, paint a picture, and start companies. But will it make an eternal difference in the lives of others? Will it be blessed by God? To make that kind of significant difference and move mountains, we don't need a shovel and talent. We need a different attitude. An attitude of reliance, dependence, expectation, and belief in the One who can move mountains, calm the seas, and use us to change our world. This is pride and self-reliance versus relying on God to work through us. When we rely on God's ability and not our capability, we can make a difference in eternity.

I've always known that badgers were ferocious creatures and supreme diggers. What I didn't know was their tenacity and willingness to tackle huge jobs no matter how long it takes. Our badger was excited about the opportunity and wanted the pleasure of feasting on the calf for weeks.

I guess it's just a matter of the prize. If we value the prize enough, we will be willing to talk to Pharaoh, sling stones at a giant, hide spies, and endure shipwrecks. As long as we rely on God's ability, we can laugh at impossibilities.

When we rely on God's ability,
we can laugh at impossibilities.

Moonlit Musings

1. What big jobs or opportunities have you been offered that you thought, "No way am I qualified for this!"
2. Have you seen others take on jobs or projects successfully that you couldn't imagine tackling?
3. Are there any dreams or projects you would love to accomplish but you don't think you're qualified? What small steps could you take to make this a reality?
4. Do you think you might now discern a prompting to complete a "God project" for which you may not feel qualified? How can you depend on God for provision?

Prayer

Heavenly Father,

Many things in my life can feel like an impossibility, and I've certainly tried to change them in my own strength! Thank you for your Word, which shows me many examples of people relying on you to equip and accomplish what they couldn't on their own. Show me where in my life I'm not relying on you. Please help me to lay down my capabilities and rely on your infallibility.

In Jesus' name, amen.

[1] James Herriot, Every Living Thing, (St. Martin's Press, 1993).

CHAPTER 6

Raccoon

BANG! The sudden explosion jolted me off the pillow. I looked at the clock—it was 2:00 a.m. What on earth had made that tremendous sound? Did something crash into the house? A car out of control? That was unlikely, we lived on a cul-de-sac. My husband was still sound asleep and I didn't hear anything from our son's room, so I was the only one to hear it. Despite the late hour, my curiosity got the best of me, and I got up to investigate.

As I padded downstairs in the hushed darkness, I thought of all those scary movies where you're thinking, "Don't go downstairs! Don't go into the basement you fool!" But the sound seemed to be outside, not inside, so I kept exploring. Nothing was out of place downstairs. No large object had fallen. I couldn't figure out what made the noise. Had I imagined it? Why did it jolt me awake and nobody else? Then I heard them.

Just outside the kitchen windows were broadcasts of squeaks, grunts, growls, snarls and otherworldly animal fighting sounds. What the heck? That sounded like a pack of 20 cats having a brawl.

I tiptoed over to the kitchen windows and looked out. Our solid, nearly 4-foot-tall trash bins had been toppled over. As I looked closer, I saw the bags had been ripped open, and garbage was spewing out everywhere. And the culprits were fighting over the spoils—raccoons!

Despite having bungee-corded the lids closed, they had managed through teamwork to tip over the heavy bins and remove the tightly fitted cords. And this wasn't the first time.

I used to put bricks and heavy objects on top of our garbage bins to prevent raccoons from getting inside. That didn't work. It was mere child's play for them to outwit me. Next, I used tighter and tighter bungee cords. Ones so tight I could barely get them on myself and feared them springing loose and blinding me as they whipsawed open. But you dare *not* find a way to close your bins; otherwise, in the morning you could be greeted with a raccoon who dove down headfirst and got stuck in there overnight. Then you had to find a way to let him loose safely.

It was getting harder and harder to outwit these var-mints and I was getting frustrated.

There's a good reason for this.

Raccoons are smarter and more adaptable than you imagine. As much as I boast about the brilliance of poo-dles and German Shepherd dogs (both breeds in our home growing up) recent intelligence tests place raccoons just under the intelligence of monkeys and ahead of dogs. And their remarkable, dexterous paws can pick locks, open windows, doors, picnic coolers and garbage cans. Native to North America, these nocturnal mammals with their ring-striped tails were called *aroughcun* by the Powhatan tribe which means "animal that scratches with its hands."

The most famous feature about raccoons is the fact they seem to "wash" their food in water. My grandmother used to put out scraps of food and a shallow pan of water at night to watch and photograph this unique behavior.

But are they really "washing" their food? While most animals use their senses of sight, sound, and smell to find food, raccoons depend on their sense of touch. Their front paws consist of five dexterous appendages that are remarkably nimble, function like human fingers, and contain about four times more sensory receptors than their back paws. This is about the same proportion in humans. This way they can discriminate items without seeing them—a helpful talent for feeding in the dark. So, what we think is washing their food, is actually dousing—wetting their paws to stimulate nerve endings. In this way, they get more sensory information about what they are handling.

Their back paws are equally impressive. They can rotate them 180 degrees, allowing them to climb up and down obstacles headfirst.

Raccoons' cute face masks make them look like quintessential thieves, but the dark coloring serves a purpose. Like professional athletes who use dark smudges around their eyes, their black mask helps absorb incoming light and reducing glare that might obstruct their vision at night.

Their thick pelts and cute faces are the reason you find them outside of North America now. In the 1920s they were exported to Europe for supplying fur farms. Calvin Coolidge, the 30th president of the United States (1923-1929) had a pet raccoon named Rebecca. At that time, it wasn't unusual to have raccoon meat on the table in America. But he decided this smart little mammal would make a great pet (alongside his bobcat, goose, donkey, wallaby and others).

Author Sterling North published *Rascal: A Memoir of a Better Era*, in 1963 about a year in his childhood in Wisconsin when he raised a baby raccoon. I read this book out loud to my son when he was young and we were both astounded and delighted at the cleverness of raccoons. (I skipped the parts about his anger at God over the death of his mother—I figured life has enough angst later on; I didn't need to introduce it so early.)

In the 1970s, Japanese children were enamored with an anime cartoon series on TV about a cuddly raccoon. Kids clamored for their own pet raccoon, so Japan imported about 1500 a month for a while. Of course, many of these pets ended up back in the wild, and Japan has now prohibited importing and owning them.

If you've ever heard and seen raccoons fighting, you'll think twice about having them as a pet. (Only 13 states allow this.) Raccoons can be frighteningly vicious and cause serious damage. They are also much more likely to carry rabies than skunks.

The reason they have been desired as pets is their intelligence and cleverness. And the reason they have not just survived but thrived in any location is their adaptability. This resilience and adaptability has also led to their increased intelligence.

Although they don't "belong" in cities, they have prospered and increased in our cement jungles. In the forest they eat birds, insects, fruits, nuts, and seeds. In the city and suburban areas they find plenty of garbage and pet food. Scientists have noticed their uncanny learning capabilities and put them to the test.

Biologist and psychologist Suzanne MacDonald at York University in Toronto placed garbage cans containing food in both rural and urban areas. The city raccoons could easily open the lids, but the country raccoons failed every time.

In the 1900s, H.B. Davis gave 12 raccoons a series of locks to figure out. To reach the treats inside boxes, they had to figure out various hooks, bolts, latches, and levers, with some boxes having more than one lock. With their dexterous hands and learning capabilities, they solved 11 of the 13 puzzles.

Today researchers have discovered raccoons were teachable in learning how to overcome obstacles to reach food with a series of steps. The raccoons surprised the researchers with their ability to cheat the system and find the food in a faster time.

In intelligence tests they found that raccoons found in nature are significantly less intelligent than their city cousins. This led to the understanding that our suburbs and cities were "training grounds" for them. As they adapted to their environment, learned new systems, and taught it to their young, they thrived.

Scientists call this evolving intelligence. Facing challenges and learning to overcome alien and unfamiliar situations expanded their mental capacities and ability to thrive. This is an attitude and approach I am striving to master.

So often in my talks with friends, we lament what we've lost. As we navigate middle age, we find ourselves saying, "I didn't used to be like this," or, "I never struggled with this before." It's as if we've found ourselves in an alien landscape and we're not sure how to steer our way through it. Our capable and strong bodies change, our relationships twist and turn, and society morphs in unexpected ways around us. We look back wistfully at the way things used to be when life was simpler, easier, and we could cruise through without a thought.

If you're like me, you might even get somewhat of an attitude about your situation and tend to learn things the hard way. During my seven years of infertility, I was not a paragon of virtue and trust in God's goodness. I struggled, swore, and was generally furious at God for placing me in that very painful and foreign land. *This isn't fair* was my constant lament. Drug addicts were having babies and throwing them in dumpsters. Why couldn't I have one? I'd certainly be a better mother!

Those painful years in an alien landscape certainly did make me a better mother. By the time I held my precious boy in my arms, I was quite willing to drop everything in my life to care for him. Gone were my notions of building my career, placing him in someone else's care for most of the day. I deeply understood the undeserved endowment and privilege of raising this gift from God. We both thrived and I look back on those child raising years with pleasure and gratitude.

I don't always choose the long, painful path to growth. Thanks to reading many biographies of people in prison camps, living in harsh and painful environments, or debilitating physical limitations, I've discovered that it is possible to adapt and grow. Blaming God and others, wishing for something other, just digs the misery hole deeper.

When I'm in the disoriented state and I start longing for what used to be, I think about the wise words of Elisabeth Elliot. "We are meddling with God's business when we let all manner of imaginings loose, predicting disaster, contemplating possibilities instead of following, one day at a time, God's plain and simple pathway...The psalmist understood this when he wrote, 'Lord, you have assigned me my portion and my cup; you have made my lot secure' (Psalm 16:5)."

I am watching friends and acquaintances lose their jobs, savings, and relationships with family members lately. They feel as if the ground is shifting beneath them and what was once familiar and solid is now feeling alien and disorientating. The political and financial news both here and around the world just exacerbates it. Both traditional and alternative news channels all convey the same message, "Expect change. Expect the unexpected."

But choosing the hard work and mental toughness of adapting and finding some reason to be grateful makes a world of difference. The old-timers called this grit. Modern jargon calls this a growth mindset. The Bible calls it wise and biblical living.

1 Thessalonians 5:18 says, "In everything give thanks. For this is God's will for you in Christ Jesus" (NET). Our eyes glaze over these words and we give mental ascent to

them. But when you're in the middle of an alien or painful situation, they seem cruel.

I think that's because we confuse the word, "in" with "for." We can be thankful "in" tough times for the blessings of family, health, or whatever comes our way to lighten the load. But as citizens of a sin-soaked world, I don't think that means "thankful for."

I'm not going to parrot that we should be thankful for cancer, heartache and other miseries that befall us. But I think we can find a way to be thankful for something, in most situations.

When my husband got laid off and discovered no one wanted to hire someone in their sixties, he pursued his passion in Artificial Intelligence and started a company. It's not wildly successful (yet) but he found that diving into something interesting and learning the latest coding languages gave him a new lease on life. He could have whimpered, wallowed into the couch, and whined that life wasn't fair. Instead, like the raccoons, he adapted to his new landscape. His growth mindset has resulted in him getting smarter and wiser about the latest technologies.

*Adaptability may be the key
to life's enjoyability.*

Those who have figured out how to stop wishing for how things used to be, or how things "ought" to be, have discovered they can recapture that ease of living from their youth. They have learned how to "cruise" through life with a joyful and carefree attitude. Like our adaptable raccoons, they have increased their intelligence to live with joy.

When we turn from sighing how life used to be, we can discover the secret to thriving in our new territory.

Jesus said, "I have come so that they may have life, and may have it abundantly" (John 10:10). When we adapt to our new circumstances, we can attract that abundant life.

Moonlit Musings

1. What have you had to adapt to in the last few years?
2. What have been your surprising new territories or most difficult things you've had to adapt to?
3. In what ways have you grown stronger and smarter thanks to these new situations?
4. Can you thank God for those gains?

Prayer

Heavenly Father,

The animal world you have created is truly extraordinary. The adaptability of raccoons to new environments is such a lesson for me. Thank you for your words of hope about having an abundant life; this is something I want to reach for. Help me stop grumbling about changes and how things used to be and start looking for ways I can adapt. I look forward to your plans for me.

In Jesus' name, amen.

CHAPTER 7

Barn Owl

The Barn Owl glided over the snow in the early morning light, his head bent down, facing the drifts. The breeze ruffled the tips of his wings, but his flight was silent. A ghostly, pale predator, he lazily looped over the field. A short distance away, a Kestrel was also soaring over the snow. They were both on the hunt for rodents that they knew to be under the white drifts. But where?

The Kestrel, accustomed to hunting in the day, seemed to have the advantage. This was his home turf. This is where he hunted frequently with his keen eyesight. Scanning the snowbanks, he thought he heard something—or maybe the snow heaved a little? He bulleted down, claws extended, only to come up empty.

Meanwhile, the Barn Owl—not used to hunting by

day but being forced to, due to bad weather—was still airborne. He tilted his odd, moon-like face and directed his ears toward the snow. He hovered in flight, tilting his head back and forth, assessing the rise beneath him. In a decisive and milky blur, he rocketed down to the snow, talons out. Despite no visible indication, he knew where the target was. Soaring back up to the treetops, he carried his prize, a mouse.

Why was the Barn Owl successful and the Kestrel wasn't? And don't owls usually hunt at night?

Barn Owls—like most owls—usually hunt after dark. But this one couldn't hunt the night before due to harsh weather, so he was forced into dealing with the bright light reflecting off the snowdrifts. Barn Owls don't store fat very well and can't hunt in severe weather (which is why their number one reason for death is starvation), so sometimes they can be seen hunting in the daylight. The Kestrel only had his eyesight. The Barn Owl used eyesight a little, but mostly his superior hearing.

Barn Owls are known to have the most acute hearing in the world of owls. They also have sharper hearing than cats or dogs. In fact, tests conducted on the audio skills of Barn Owls show that they can locate their prey in complete darkness—as if they are blindfolded.

I've always loved owls. Nothing beats hearing the lonesome, wild hoot of a Great Horned Owl in the middle of the night. Long-eared Owls always look surprised and cute. Burrowing owls look totally irritated with their perpetual funny frown, but the Barn Owl? He's an anomaly. He's the odd, ghost-like bird of the night.

Barn Owls have an almost alien appearance. Their white

heart-shaped face resembles an Elizabethan collar around their dark eyes. Splitting the face in two is a long, white nose—giving them a look utterly different from most North American owls. They have primarily white breasts with tawny, cream, and grey mottled feathers.

They don't have a charming hoot like the Great Horned Owl either. Their vocalizations are hissing and a rough, unnerving screech, like a frail woman's scream.

Like all owls, his flight is as silent as falling snow. This is due to the owl's feather structure, which eliminates sound when he flies. To have an owl soar unexpectedly over your head at twilight is a startling and somewhat spooky experience.

Barn Owls are so named because that's where they are most comfortable—up in the rafters of a barn. This is because their diet is made up of little rodents that are abundant on farms: voles, moles, gophers, and mice. Also, when the weather is harsh, he can hunt for critters rustling around in the hay within the barn. The Barn Owl's constitution for rough weather is not as resilient as the stout Great Horned Owl. So he needs to be in a barn or nesting box. In addition, if you put out poison for rats and other rodents, you are also poisoning Barn Owls, since they eat those dead rodents. It is best to put up Barn Owl nesting boxes on nearby trees if you want to rid your place of rodents. No barn is needed.

So how is the Barn Owl's hearing superior to other owls for catching all these rodents? First, his face is shaped like a satellite disk, and the ruff around the edges directs and focuses the sound. But most striking are his ears, which are hidden under feathers like most owls. They are asymmetrical. One is higher on his head than the other. The left ear captures sounds and rustlings below, while the right ear focuses on sounds above. Also, one ear is slightly more forward-facing. This difference in ear positions means the owl will hear a sound at two slightly different times. This difference is only 3 microseconds, but it enables him to pinpoint his prey with a three-dimensional auditory map. The owl can determine not only the direction of a sound but also its height and distance.

Scientists in 1958 were the first to document and demonstrate the ability of the Barn Owl to locate mice acoustically in total darkness. Also, it was noted that a Barn Owl will not strike sounds new to it (paper rustling, for instance), but it can quickly learn slight differences between sounds that bring reward vs. no reward.

In 2017, the Royal Society of Great Britain published a paper demonstrating that not only do owls have acute hearing, but their ability to hear does not diminish with age. Think about the older family dog. As he ages, he no longer jumps up and barks at kids down the street or the mailbox lid opening next to the front door. Dogs' hearing diminishes with age, but not with Barn Owls. In fact, right up until death, the Barn Owl's hearing remains acute.

This is definitely not true for me. While I wouldn't say I need hearing aids yet, I do manage to misconstrue what I hear. The other day, I had a bizarre hearing mishap with my husband. We were walking back from a couple's Bible study where one of the women—a former Air Force pilot—had presented some ideas that were striking in their thoughtfulness. We were talking about how kind and thoughtful her responses usually were. What I heard Tom say was, "She has Marxist tendencies."

I looked at him, confused. "Marxist? How can you call her a Marxist? With her background in the Air Force, I'm pretty sure she's not a Marxist!" Now, it was Tom's turn to look confused.

"Laurie," he said, "I said she has marks of stability. Not Marxist tendencies!"

Oh. Well then!

While this example of mishearing causes hilarity in the retelling, it also shows how badly we can misconstrue what we hear. This happens in the spiritual realm as well.

In the 1970s and 80s, a popular booklet or tract emphasizing spiritual laws was published. Evangelists handed these out to help people understand the gospel (or "good news") of Jesus giving us new life. I first saw one on campus at my university.

It had a tidy, 4-step process of how to come to know God. And the first point read, "God loves you and has a wonderful plan for your life." What my ears heard from point one was basically the "prosperity gospel." Meaning, a wonderful plan certainly meant health, wealth, friends, and no serious problems. Anyone who has circled the sun for more than a few decades can see the fallacy of this belief. And when reality bumps up against what we believe we've heard about or from God, disappointment and bitterness can result.

A well-intentioned relative told me, "God helps those who help themselves." I thought that was a verse in the Bible. I heard it as, "God is there, but you pretty much need to bootstrap it and not rely on Him." This is antithetical to God's nature, and it's not in the Bible. My hearing and belief system were skewed, and my attitude and life decisions reflected that faulty thinking.

⁂

When our hearing is contorted,
it's hard to get our lives sorted.

⁂

Sharpening our hearing is of primary importance regarding matters of faith. Jesus emphasized this as well. As He was walking in the temple one day, religious leaders and faithful Jews asked him, "How long will you keep us in suspense? If you are the Messiah, tell us plainly." Jesus answered, "I did tell you, but you do not believe. The works I do in my Father's name testify about me, but you do not believe because you are not my sheep. My sheep listen to my voice; I know them, and they follow me. I give them eternal life, and they shall never perish; no one will snatch them out of my hand" (John 10:24-28).

The religious leaders claimed they wanted to hear and understand, but their ears were blocked. Maybe they were blocked by prejudice? (What can anyone from Nazareth—that backwater town—know?) Maybe preconceived notions about the Messiah? (Surely the Messiah would overthrow the Romans?) Maybe pride? (Surely, this humble carpenter cannot be our Messiah!) Whatever the reasons, they didn't have "ears to hear" (Mark 4:9).

So, how do we open up our spiritual ears to hear what God would say to us? So many voices, videos, "experts," and noises are pouring into our ears daily. How do we discern that which is from God vs. the world's opinions? And especially when we are groping through the darkest moments in our lives, we desperately need to hear from God. How does this happen?

I've heard this next Bible verse so many times over the years. But lately, as I've gotten older and faced those long, lonely, dark nights in life I come back to its wisdom and surety.

> "So then faith comes by hearing, and hearing by the word of God" (Romans 10:17 NKJV).

Notice the repetition of "hearing, and hearing"? It's not a one-time experience. It's an ongoing practice. Hearing, and hearing, and hearing throughout our lives. Hearing what? Hearing the Word of God—the Bible.

The English Standard Version puts it this way:

> "So faith comes from hearing, and hearing through the word of Christ."

I have to be reminded of the Truth over and over when I'm groping around in the dark. Sometimes, this is a friend pointing me back to where wisdom is found. Sometimes, this is my husband reminding me of what God's Word says versus my opinions and experiences. My experiences and senses tell me one thing, but God's Word is an immovable and sure homing device, discernable through the darkest moments.

There is much darkness in our world today. And many voices are claiming to point the way. But there is One voice we can tune our sheepish ears to hear. The voice of our faithful Shepherd. Only He can lead us out of the darkness to a place where we have no lack.

The Barn Owl can find what he needs in total darkness because of his acute hearing. Although we may feel surrounded and suffocated by the growing gloom, we can stop, tilt our heads, and listen intently. We can seize upon His Word and find our sustenance. We can find a way through the darkest times and face the future with new strength and hope. Then darkness has no claim over us.

Moonlit Musings

1. Have you heard any common statements (like, "God helps those who help themselves") that you believed?
2. What things in your life do you think dull your ears to God's voice? Or to His Word?
3. Which of these Bible truths could you hold onto and repeat to yourself in the dark times?
4. When do you feel most open to hearing God? At night in bed? Outside on a walk? Listening to music?

Prayer

Heavenly Father,

Thank you for not leaving me in silence. You gave me your Word to guide me. I'm so grateful for the power of your words. "For the word of God is alive and active. Sharper than any double-edged sword, it penetrates even to dividing soul and spirit, joints and marrow; it judges the thoughts and attitudes of the heart" (Hebrews 4:12). Please give me a supernatural hunger for your truth revealed in the Bible. And show me any common misbeliefs I have taken on as my own. I want to be led by you, not by popular culture or opinion.

In Jesus' name, amen.

CHAPTER 8

Mushrooms

The spring rain patters softly down onto the forest floor. Water drips off the massive oak and fir tree limbs and splatters onto last year's brown leaves. The air is sharp with the tang of evergreen and wet earth. Nearby a tiny stream gurgles with the fresh introduction of rain. A salamander slinks through the dead leaves and needles on his way to the vernal pool, which fills with life-giving water on spring evenings like this. In the misty gloom of night, something else is stirring on the forest floor.

Underneath the pine needles and tree roots, a long conversation has been taking place. It has been going on for years—sometimes hundreds or thousands of years. A dense network of communication lines has been shuttling information from tree to tree and plant to plant. It is all connected to one giant web of circuitry similar to that of the internet, with more networks than our brains have of neural pathways. And with every step above ground, underneath is 300 miles of a dense fungi network of tiny filaments called mycelium.

This mycelium is the support structure for keeping our forests healthy. Its thread-like, branching tendrils shuttle nutrients to ailing trees, signal when pests are about, and stabilize and store carbon. It is one of nature's most resilient organisms, being both fire-resistant and water-retardant. It also produces fruit—fungi—in the form of mushrooms. These mushrooms are the forest's digestive track or clean-up crew.

By ingesting nutrients from the decomposing plant material and re-dispersing them to other plants and trees via the mycelium, life happens. Without them, our forests would choke with dead animals, trees, and leaves, crowding out all new growth.

Mushrooms are the fruiting body of the rarely seen but immense mycelium network. And scientists are now discovering the amazing soil-healing and regenerating properties of mushrooms in the environment.

Paul Stamets, mushroom explorer, scientist, and businessman, reported on the remarkable capabilities of mushrooms to heal soil ruined by diesel and other petroleum wastes in a TED talk. He reports:

> "There were 4 piles saturated with diesel and other petroleum waste. One was a control pile, one pile was treated with enzymes, one pile treated with bacteria, and our pile we inoculated with mushroom spores. . .When we returned 6 weeks later, all the tarps were

removed, all these other piles were dead, dark, and stinky. We come back to our pile and it is covered with hundreds of pounds of oyster mushrooms. . . And something else happened, which is an epiphany in my life. The fungi sporulated the spores then attracted insects, birds then came bringing in seeds, and our pile became an oasis of life."

After the devastating wildfires on the West Coast, the environmental toxic load was immense. It wasn't just trees that burned. When every house went up in flames, so did cleaning products, fertilizers, electronics, paint, plastics, and a multitude of other noxious items. This left behind arsenic, asbestos, lead, and more pollutants. When rain follows, what then? It seeps down into our drinking water and washes into waterways filled with fish, shellfish, and plant life.

In Sonoma County, fire remediation experts, local businesses, and ecological activists joined together to help clean up the toxic mess created by the wildfires. They packed over 40 miles of wattles (a tube-shaped erosion control device that is used to slow or stop water flow in areas with slopes or ditches) with straw, set them up for erosion control, and inoculated them all with oyster mushroom spores. Thus, runoff was diverted away from threatened waterways, and the mushrooms aided in further absorption of the toxins.

Five years after the Chernobyl nuclear disaster, mycelium and mushrooms were found on the walls of the nuclear reactor in 1991. We currently have no viable methods of reversing radioactive devastation, which makes these kinds of fungi, which can mineralize radionuclides from their environment and incorporate it into their own biomass, a beacon of hope.

Mushrooms are not only life-giving to the landscape, but they also do the same for the body.

I had my own surprising encounter with the power of mushrooms with my doctor. While she was reviewing my yearly blood levels she remarked, "Wow! Your vitamin D levels are great! I don't usually see this. What do you do—spend a lot of time in the sun?" I looked at her surprised. It was winter. And although we are in California, 50-degree days full of rain didn't warrant a lot of sunbathing.

"No," I replied. She looked at me, tilted her head and asked, "Do you eat a lot of mushrooms?" I brightened, "Oh yes! I have them almost every morning with eggs. I love them. But what does that have to do with vitamin D?"

"Mushrooms are *full* of vitamin D," she said. Who knew? Something that grew in the dark, and feasted on lifeless matter was somehow able to transfer the life-giving benefits of sunshine to my body. I was enchanted.

We see a pattern here. A pattern of waste conversion. That the fungi—or mushrooms—can decompose dead things, grow in the dark—sometimes overnight—and yet heal soil, give life, transfer nutrients, and rejuvenate other living things. How fascinating that the life-giving properties of fungi is discovered on things that are dying and decaying. This is a pattern that God has set out from the beginning.

꙳ ⋅ ꙳

*God is the Divine Alchemist; He will take
the death of our plans and dreams
and cause new life to spring forth.*

꙳ ⋅ ꙳

It comforts me to know that when plans, projects, or even people crumble and fall apart, there is the possibility of rejuvenation and resurrection around the corner. That, contrary to appearances, it is not all for nothing. God can take our cherished dreams, and although they seem lost to us—or maybe even torn from our clenched fists—turn them into something beautiful and life-giving. The Creator of our world is the Divine Alchemist. He delights in taking our failures, heartaches, treasured talismans, and anything we value above Him, into a hope and future that doesn't disappoint. But it comes at a cost.

Today, the pithy messages of "Jesus and a cup of coffee" or, "Jesus is my boyfriend" shrink, devalue, and demean the miraculous transformation He offers on the other side of death. And that's the keyword: death. The very thing we find repugnant, we repel from and reject. As the old saying goes, "Everyone wants to go to heaven, but nobody wants to die." Yet, the only way we see the alchemy of loss and failure turn to hope and life is through the portal of death.

This can mean relinquishment or death to our plans, our dreams, or sometimes our very lives. Without a rock-solid theology based on experiential knowledge of the love of God, it can feel capricious, cruel, and somewhat crazy. But it is the only doorway.

I read many biographies because I find them fascinating, and I derive strength and hope for my journey by reading about the struggles of others. How did Corrie ten Boom survive the Nazi death camps—and the death of her beloved sister—without rage and bitterness towards her captors? How did Elisabeth Elliot go back and serve the Ecuadorian natives who butchered her husband? How did she then survive the death of her second husband to cancer without resentment towards God? How did Katie Davis reject the privilege of her upper-class teenage life of new cars, dating, and popularity and die to that promised "good life" to live in Uganda and establish an orphanage? All of these people died to—or relinquished—their cherished dreams and plans. Why? How? Because they surrendered it all. They laid it down. They had been crucified.

"I have been crucified with Christ and I no longer live, but Christ lives in me. The life I now live in the body, I live by faith in the Son of God, who loved me and gave himself for me" said the apostle Paul in the book of Galatians (Gal 2:20). Paul, who was a brilliant scholar and devout Christian killer, had been utterly changed by his encounter with Jesus. He relinquished his own fame within the religious circles. He died to his own plans. He set aside what he thought was the right path for his life. This is the path we must choose if we want to see a true, vibrant life beyond what we could imagine for ourselves.

Jesus said, "I am the way and the truth and the life. No one comes to the Father but through me" (John 14:6). In a world of options, opinions, and morphing personal truths, this is a hard stop. It's not about "being spiritual" or religious. It's not about church attendance, membership, or even belief in historical facts. It's about dying to self and being transformed by Him. And it's a narrow gate.

I desperately want to be the darling of the New York Times Book Review and make enough money to live out my dreams, be interviewed on NPR, buy a house, etc. However, although the Bible's truths are not popular—they won't get me on any talk shows—they are true. And like the package states on Hebrew National hot dogs, "We report to a higher authority." Therefore, I can't soft-pedal it. I can't escape what Jesus said, no matter how much it grates my notions of spirituality, inclusivity, fairness, or beliefs: "Enter through the narrow gate. For wide is the gate and broad is the road that leads to destruction, and many enter through it. But small is the gate and narrow the road that leads to life, and only a few find it" (Matthew 7:13,14).

Much of what we see today in the media of people calling themselves Christian is the complete opposite of this. We see people's faces contorted with rage, demanding their rights, spreading heresy, hate, gossip, and rumors, asking for money, and generally just being jerks. To be clear, this is politically on both sides of the aisle. This behavior does not speak of that narrow way. We need discernment. We need to remember His words, "By their fruits you will know them" (Matthew 7:20).

"But what about my dreams?" you are thinking. "What about the wrongs I suffered? How do I 'die' to all this and get the rebirth, renewal, and better life you are alluding to here? How do I just let go of all the tragedy and disappointment that has landed in my lap?"

I'm not the suffering and death expert, although my struggles loom large in my life, they would probably seem minuscule to you. But I do struggle with bitterness, rage, feeling left out, that maybe God loves others more than me, etc. That's why I read those biographies. That's why I read the Bible (plenty of suffering and struggling there). They are all signposts, part of the great web of truth that communicates the same message: let it go.

Pray for strength to do this. Pray for faith to trust God. Let it all drop to the earth and die. Let it decay, get swallowed up, and watch God's alchemy take place. Wait in anticipation and trust for something better to push up through that darkness.

Despite the horrors of Nazi death camps, Corrie ten Boom discovered the miraculous power and peace of forgiveness. So did Elisabeth Elliot (as well as unwavering trust in God's goodness). Katie Davis is tasting the joy and thrill of watching God deliver miraculous answers to needs beyond her ability to fulfill (like feeding and housing her 13 adopted children).

This is the whole message of God's gorgeous, lush world that nature lovers delight in: death, decay, new life. And this is not just for the great hereafter or heavenly vistas. This is for here. For now. For your life.

The apostle John recorded Jesus' words that do away with any notion of a stern God wanting His followers to live lives full of suffering and misery with no hope of rebirth or joy.

> "I came that they may have life, and have it abundantly" (John 10:10 NASB).

Jesus set the example for us by giving up His life. Why do we think we have a better plan? Relinquish those things He is gently trying to tug from your hands. Die to it all, let it decay, and watch that abundant life—like so many thriving mushrooms on decomposing matter—surge forth, surprise, and delight you. And you will thrive.

Moonlit Musings

1. What dreams or desires did you have that came to nothing or maybe even were taken away from you?
2. Have you watched someone suffer from the loss of something great, but do so with a surprisingly good attitude?
3. What areas of your life—or dreams—do you think you might have a too-tight hold on?
4. Have you seen new and better life sprout from things that seemed like an awful loss at the moment, like loss of a job, position, or relationship?

Prayer

Heavenly Father,

Your world is fascinating! I am so thankful that you have a system for taking dead things in nature and having them facilitate life. I need this in my life as well. Please give me the courage to let go where I need to let go and trust you to create something better out of my decaying dreams and plans. Help me wait expectantly for your plans of growth to emerge.

In Jesus' name, amen.

CHAPTER 9

Sea Turtle

I n slow motion, the sea turtle rises from the depths to gulp some air between the ocean swells. It's been a long journey. Some years, she swims across oceans up to 12,000 miles, a migration surpassed only by whales. But this year, she has serenely swum from the bracing waves of North America, where she foraged on jellyfish, through the Sargasso Sea and down to the sultry climes of the Caribbean.

It has taken decades for her to reach sexual maturity. Only 1 in 1000 survive to attain this milestone. She is headed back to the *natal* beach where she was born. Like salmon, sea turtles migrate thousands of miles of oceanic currents and tides to return to their place of birth. Current research suggests they navigate this via the earth's magnetic fields.

Our Leatherback sea turtle has traveled farther than any other sea turtle in the world. Heavy with the weight of eggs, she lumbers through the breaking waves to the shoreline.

As the largest of the sea turtles, this Leatherback is about six feet long and weighs 2,000 pounds. Her leathery shell—which, unlike other sea turtles, isn't a hard shell—is what gives her, her name. Long raised lines, like the keel on a boat, stripe down her back, making her highly hydro-dynamic in her aquatic environment.

But on land, she is an enormous, ungainly behemoth, ill-suited for moving on sand. Slowly, she hefts her bulk up on the beach, pushing herself forward with her enormous front flippers. Once she reaches the high tide mark, she begins to dig.

Using her back flippers, she patiently flips sand away from her back end until she has dug a pit 30 inches deep. Now, the egg-laying begins.

She drops about 100 wet and shiny globes into the cool pit. In fact, the temperature of this sandy incubator will determine the sex of her baby turtles. If it's mostly cool, the result will be predominately male turtles. If, however, the sand is warmer over the next 55-60 days of incubation, the result will be primarily female turtles.

Now, she carefully covers up her nest of eggs with sand to prevent raccoons, foxes, seagulls, and other predators from reaching her precious cargo.

Exhausted, she must now heave her prodigious weight back across the sand. Hopefully, she can do this before the sun comes up. Otherwise, as the sun heats up the sand, it will become harder and harder for her to make it, as increasing heat can sometimes become lethal.

Scrape, heave, pant. Scrape, heave, pant. Slowly, she makes her way back to her watery home. Once there, the cool waters wash over her, and she is free. Effortlessly, she glides through the water to forage for another 10 days until she repeats the nest-making process. She will do this 7-10 times over the season. After her last nesting period, she begins her migration across oceans to other foraging grounds around the world. She will spend 3-4 years feeding to build up enough energy to nest again.

Leatherback sea turtles are not the only ones that traverse the oceans and lay their eggs on beaches. Loggerheads, Hawksbill, and other sea turtles go through the same journey as our Leatherback, although not as far. But they all need clean, protected beaches to lay their eggs in.

Loggerhead sea turtles are named for their overly large heads; you can find them throughout the world's oceans. They are the largest of the hard-shelled sea turtles, with adults reaching between 300 and 400 pounds. Unlike Leatherbacks, they have powerful jaws that crack open hard-shelled mollusks, crabs, shrimp, and the occasional jellyfish.

Green sea turtles are not green. But because they eat exclusively algae, kelp, and sea grasses, their subcutaneous fat is green. And this is why fishing trawlers using chain-weighted nets are so disastrous; they rip out meadows of seagrass that our sea turtles and many fish rely on.

The Hawksbill sea turtle is named for its hawk-like beak. These turtles are the ones with beautiful shells, which are most likely harvested for tortoiseshell jewelry and trinkets. In fact, these turtles have been nearly wiped out due to poaching and overharvesting for their decorative shells.

Most people are unfamiliar with the Olive Ridley sea turtle, but they do have a remarkable nesting habit. Unlike our Leatherback, which nests privately and singularly, the Olive Ridley sea turtle nests with her buddies—thousands of them at once, on the same beach.

While all sea turtles migrate impressive distances around the world's oceans, none are as large nor travel as far as the Leatherback.

Since all sea turtles are air-breathing reptiles, they must survive coming to the surface in open oceans as they swim across. Therefore, they are in danger of boat strikes, orcas, and sharks killing them.

Unlike freshwater turtles that can fully retract their heads and limbs into their protective shells, sea turtles cannot. But they do have a neat trick that our land-dwelling turtles do not. Sea turtles can hold their breath for an impressive amount of time, between 4–7 hours when resting. While they do this, their heart rate slows considerably to conserve oxygen—up to 9 minutes between heartbeats.

Our Leatherback loves jellyfish, and if you've ever been stung by one snorkeling, you want this sea turtle around. But don't they get stung as well? Nope. Their beaks and shells protect them from stings. The spiny growths called *papillae* provide a type of armor from their esophagus down to the stomach. This is the same material as human fingernails and hair. A thick layer protects the turtle from stings in their throat or stomach.

Tragically, plastic bags floating in the ocean and undulating with the waves and currents look just like jellyfish to a sea turtle. Once ingested, they block their digestive tract and kill the sea turtles. (This is why I'm a fan of reusable, latex bags like Stasher™ instead of Ziplocks™.)

But back to our baby turtles. They have been under the sand, developing for about two months. Now, they are beginning to break out of their shells. Everyone in the nest emerges out of their shells at the same time. But they wait under the sand, just up under the surface, until they can feel that the sand has cooled. This indicates safety. It means it is probably nighttime, and they have a chance to scramble out under the cover of darkness and make it into the water.

Once out of the nest, they must squirm and wiggle past a gauntlet of hungry seabirds, crabs, foxes, raccoons, and other predators eager for this easy meal.

The first few break through the surface, and it is nighttime. A perfect time to escape to the sea. They are safe to make their frantic trip to the water. Or are they?

Turtles are phototactic (attracted to light). So our baby Leatherbacks are following the moon's light over the water which is beckoning them to safety, thus they are scrambling after its light—which should be the moon's light.

Tragically, thanks to modern electricity so close to the beaches where they hatch, thousands of baby turtles will be lured to their deaths following the false lights of headlights from cars, city lights, or even tourists' flashlights.

Our baby Leatherbacks scrabble out of their nest, frantically climbing over each other, flailing, scrambling, and exhausting themselves, heading towards the light they think will lead them to safety and their watery destiny. Some make it into the ocean, but too many are lured off track. They end up crushed under the wheels of cars, sidelined on the sidewalks, or exhausted until they die from spending all their energy going in the wrong direction.

Scientists estimate that only about 1% of hatchlings from a nest make it to adulthood. Predators waiting on the beach for them to emerge nab many for a quick meal. False lights imitating the moon cause the rest to wander off course and die, chasing the light that never delivers them home.

Baby sea turtles aren't the only ones exhausting themselves, flailing and following false lights they believe will lead them to safety and deliver them home.

Our Inboxes are filled with promises of advancement. If I choose *this* app, program, course, or product, I will find myself successful, rich, influencing thousands, or whatever the current promise is. I know this because I have signed up for more courses than I want to admit. I may have learned a few things, but none delivered the arrival I was hungering for. None were the light that led me to my desired destination.

It's hard today to resist these twinkling lights that promise so much. We all want to feel significant, capable and liked. And it takes a lot of willpower to see these promises for what they actually are: false beacons of hope appealing to our need to find the light to bring us to our goal.

It is even more difficult to ignore these lights when you are encouraged by everyone around you to follow them. Many would-be authors are discouraged from pursuing their dreams because publishers want them to have tens of thousands of followers or a similar-sized email list. This way, publishing companies are guaranteed sales. So, authors are encouraged to spend time on social media, getting noticed, and building up a following. And then they are like our baby turtles, chasing the light of fame, completely off track, and not writing down their stories.

I heard the *Writing Off Social* podcast hosts describe it something like this: "When you are clamoring to be noticed in this noisy environment, it's like you are in a giant stadium, and everyone is yelling at the top of their voice. How on earth will you stand out in all that bawling madness?" Indeed.

This applies to everyone, not just authors. Artists, musicians, hairstylists, veterinarians, companies, and even your local dog walker are all encouraged to seize the crowd's attention, get noticed, *and build a brand!*

I get this. My background is in marketing and advertising, so I understand this outlook. But I find it an exhausting, creativity-draining, and soul-sucking pursuit.

I say I want a closer relationship with God, but then I chase after foreign beacons. As a person who seeks to emulate Jesus Christ, this should cause me some consternation. He tells me to focus on the opposite. He says I should pursue humility, service, and love. That these are the lights that will lead me home.

These are not the sexy, alluring lights of fame, but they will deliver what I hunger for.

Matthew recorded Jesus' words to the crowds regarding worrying about their daily lives. He encouraged them to pursue the Father's will. "But seek first his kingdom and his righteousness, and all these things will be given to you as well" (Matthew 6:33).

I like how Eugene Peterson's paraphrase of the Bible, *The Message,* puts it: "What I'm trying to do here is to get you to relax, to not be so preoccupied with getting, so you can respond to God's giving. People who don't know God and the way he works fuss over these things; but you know both God and how he works. Steep your life in God-reality, God-initiative, God-provisions. Don't worry about missing out. You'll find all your everyday human concerns will be met" (Matthew 6:32-33).

⁂

Scrambling after false lights in order to be known leaves us exhausted, empty, and far from our true home.

⁂

If I'm honest with myself, that's the core of my desire to chase after the wrong lights—the fear of missing out. I'm afraid others will scramble ahead of me. The whole pile will happily step on me, run ahead, and get what I want. But will I miss out? Maybe the path of humility, putting others first, and not hungering after their lives is the way home.

Maybe God Himself is my home?

I have to reorient myself when I'm tossed and turned around after chasing the false lights that promise me deliverance. I find scriptures like these keep me focused on the right light source.

"The eternal God is your refuge, and underneath are the everlasting arms" (Deuteronomy 33:27).

"Do nothing out of selfish ambition or vain conceit. Rather, in humility value others above yourselves, not looking to your own interests but each of you to the interests of the others" (Philippians 2:3).

When I meditate on these verses, I stop flailing and

scrambling after false lights. I come to the One who is the Light of the World and I am delivered from myself and false promises. He loves me to the moon and back. And I am home.

Moonlit Musings

1. Have you ever seen salmon or turtles coming back to their place of birth? (There are vacation/travel companies that allow you to participate—look it up.)
2. In what circumstances do you feel like you are competing with a crowd of others? (They may be seen or unseen.)
3. Are there any false lights you have chased after, hoping they'd deliver on promises of fulfillment?
4. Which of the verses in this chapter help you get re-orientated the most?

Prayer

Heavenly Father,

Thank you that I don't have to chase after anything but you. In you, I can find healing from heartache, peace for my path, and wisdom for my work. Please show me what false lights I may be chasing after in my life. Help me to remember, "Every good thing given and every perfect gift is from above, coming down from the Father of lights, with whom there is no variation or shifting shadow" (James 1:17 NASB).

In Jesus' name, amen.

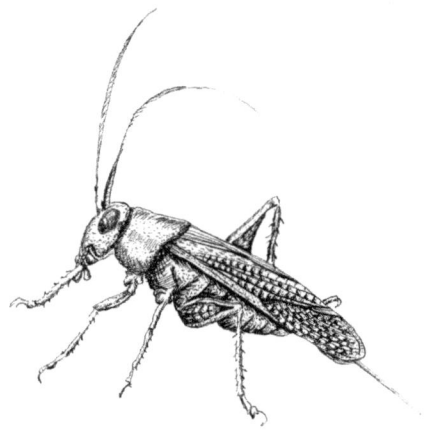

CHAPTER 10

Cricket

O utside my bedroom window, the sky was a quiet, velvet navy with just a few stars visible. The elm trees whispered in the night air. The buzzing of boats across the lake had ceased. The Blue Jays in the lilac tree below the window had settled down. The sound of the TV downstairs had been turned off an hour ago. And my book had slid onto the floor next to my bed.

As my eyelids drooped and thoughts about swimming the next day rippled through my mind, I heard the orchestra tuning up. Like a tiny band of happy chirps, the crickets began their rhythmic chirping music. In fact, the collective noun for crickets is called an *orchestra* of crickets.

There are some sounds you welcome on a hot, mid-western summer night, and some you don't. A mosquito buzzing your ear while you try to fall asleep? Definitely not. Wind sighing in the trees? Yes, please. And if you're blessed with perfect weather and you can have the window open, you'll be treated to the quintessential summer sound of crickets.

Crickets are distantly related to grasshoppers, and although they look similar—and are close in size—there are some key differences. Grasshoppers are green or brown; crickets are black or brown. Grasshoppers are strictly herbivores; they only eat plants. Crickets are omnivores; they eat other bugs as well as plants. Both can jump, but a grasshopper's range is about 2.5 feet, while the smaller cricket can leap 3 feet.

A quick way to tell the difference is that a grasshopper's antennae are stubby and short, while the cricket's antennae are quite long—as long as his body. Both insects chirp, but a grasshopper makes his music with a hind leg rubbing on a wing, while the cricket rubs both his wings together to make music. But if you're dozing at night with the window open, the chirping sound you hear is not grasshoppers because only crickets are nocturnal. They are the ones tuning up their wings to attract mates.

If you're having difficulty drifting off to sleep, you can do some cricket math in your head. Crickets chirp at different rates depending on the temperature. Most species chirp at higher rates the higher the temperature is. This relationship between temperature and the rate of chirping is known as Dolbear's law. According to this law, you can count the number of chirps produced in 15 seconds, add 40, and this will tell you the approximate temperature in degrees Fahrenheit. Some state the formula as this:

Temperature (F) = number of cricket chirps in 15 seconds + 40.

Or, if you're more science-minded, you'll be fascinated to know that there are over 900 species of crickets in the world, and every one of these has its own unique chirp. Some experts can tell which species is in an area just by listening to their music. So, how do they make their music?

Each cricket has a wing with 50-300 "teeth" set in a comb-like pattern. Crickets rub this comb area against the upper edge of its other wing. As their wing brushes their "teeth," it makes a chirping sound. Only male crickets do this, and they make their music for the same reasons most animals do—to attract and enchant the females, and to ward off rivals.

But when I'm drifting off to slumber on a summer night, the last thing I want to do is math in my head, or contemplate scientific facts. I just want to be enveloped in the sound of the happy crickets out there under the starlight, in the grass, and under the leaf litter, singing their collective aria to summer nights.

I'm not the only one who finds this sound happy. For centuries, crickets have been symbols of good luck in certain cultures. Native Americans believed crickets brought good luck, and the Chinese even more so. The Chinese believe that bringing a cricket in a charming miniature cage to the owners of a new home portends good luck. Supposedly, crickets were also used as "watchdogs" because when danger approached, the cricket would stop chirping.

Even the Bible seems to favor our happy little chirper. Leviticus 11:20, 21 states:

"All flying insects that walk on all fours are to be regarded as unclean by you. There are, however, some flying insects that walk on all fours that you may eat: those that have jointed legs for hopping on the ground. Of these you may eat any kind of locust, katydid, cricket or grasshopper."

In some Asian countries—Cambodia, Laos, and Thailand—they take this to heart. Crickets and grasshoppers are sold at street food markets deep fried and on skewers for a popular snack. There are 20,000 farmers in Thailand rearing crickets to produce 7,500 tons a year. These crickets are not only deep-fried snacks; they are also milled into flour and are increasingly used in protein bars, pet foods, and livestock feed.

This good will towards crickets has a long history in both Japan and China. While their song is common in summer and fall, it is in the winter that their music is valued as precious. So, November to January is the high season for the cricket business. This practice of securing crickets for their happy song saw its zenith in the Chun Qui period (770-476 BC) when ladies of the palace would catch crickets and place them in intricate cages so to keep chirping companions close at hand.

These cricket cages were gorgeous and charming. Made from bamboo, cloisonné, bone, carved rosewood, or even gold, they were delicate little houses of a mere few inches of artwork for their singing pets. A quick online glance will show you modern and vintage adorable cricket houses. I had to stop myself from clicking on one for eighty dollars just because I thought it was so charming.

The endearing cricket is featured in ancient poetry as well as modern literature. William Wordsworth and John Keats celebrated the cricket in poetry. Charles Dickens wrote a novella in 1845 titled, *The Cricket on the Hearth*. There is a talking cricket in *The Adventures of Pinocchio*. Then, there is my favorite, by George Selden, *The Cricket in Times Square*.

My young son and I were so taken by the story of Chester the cricket and his companions in New York City that we did a little self-styled literature tour while visiting one summer. Since we had read about Balto, the famous sled dog, and E.B. White's *Stuart Little*, we visited all the sites and statues in New York related to these wonderful children's books.

We decided we would retrace the steps of the boy Mario and his pet cricket Chester in Times Square. We hopped on the subway and made it to the Times Square station. There was no signage like you have in London's train station at platform 9 ¾ in reference to Harry Potter books, but it was special to us just the same.

At this location is where Mario, minding his father's newsstand, heard the soft, sweet chirps of Chester the cricket amongst all the bustling noises of New York. Although he was used to the honking of taxis, the rumble of the subways, and the shuffling and chattering of crowds, Mario recognized the cricket's music as something totally different and sweet. Something that reminded him of summer days lounging in the grass while visiting a friend on Long Island.

While I am charmed by stories of sweet cricket friends and the thought of palace ladies wanting crickets for the companionship of their song, I was not so charmed when I woke up to one in my home.

It's one thing to have a chorus outside, creating a backdrop for slumber; it was another thing to have that insistent chirp inside the house. I cannot sleep if there is a ticking clock, random drips from the faucet, or any sound that isn't a constant, like a fan. Irritated, I got up to find my noise maker.

I had to stand still and wait for him to chirp. Then I crept towards the sound. But of course, the nearer you get to them, the quieter they become. This is because their "ears" are actually in their legs. Crickets have an auditory organ called a tympanum located on their forelegs. This organ is hypersensitive to vibrations, which keeps them alert to approaching predators. Therefore it's pretty difficult to sneak up on a cricket. Eventually, I found him hiding behind a wastebasket under a crumpled sheet that had missed its mark.

Although I had to admit he was sweet, somehow, the minute you find one in your bedroom uninvited, your perspective changes. It becomes a *bug*, not a cute cricket that brings good luck. It morphs into being a pest, not a blessing. Invited guest and in a charming cage? He's adorable. Uninvited? He's a nuisance and not welcome. Perspective is what shifts him from companion to irritation.

I wanted to view him like the wise old Chinese man Sai Fong in *The Cricket in Times Square*. Mario travels to Chinatown to find a shop to buy a cricket cage for his new friend Chester. Outside a musty, disheveled storefront, he sees Sai Fong smoking a long clay pipe. The older man invites Mario inside to discuss crickets and find him a cage. Then Sai Fong tells him a story about why crickets are so special.

He talks about a wise man named Hsi Shuai who "spoke

only tluth." (This book was written in the 1960s, so you're going to have to put up with some cultural depictions of Chinese people who aren't able to pronounce their "r's.")

Hsi Shuai knew the thoughts of animals and men; he knew the desires of flowers and trees and the destiny of the sun and stars. And the high gods who lived in the palace at the summit of heaven loved Hsi Shuai because of the truth he spoke.

But other men did not like this. They didn't like that he exposed what was in their hearts, so they set out to kill him. Hsi Shuai knew they wanted to kill him, but he didn't care. He had peace, and he waited. Sai Fong continued the story:

"But high gods, who live in palace at summit of heaven, would not let Hsi Shuai be killed. More plecious to them than kings was this one man who only spoke tluth. So when wicked men laise swords above Hsi Shuai, high gods change him into clicket. And man who only spoke tluth and knew all things now sings songs that no man undelstands and all men love. But high gods undelstand, and smile. For to them beautiful song of clicket is song of one who still speaks tluth and knows all things." [1]

I wanted to see my cricket as the singer of a beautiful song that speaks truth. It is such a charming story that it harkens to the story of Christ, who only spoke the truth, and men wanted to kill Him for it. I struggled with resenting his song that intruded upon and disturbed my night and wanting to embrace it. This is the struggle that we all have to deal with at some point.

As long as we have God in our charming, church cage and celebrate Him on weekends, or at least Christmas and

Easter, He's in His place. Controlled, safe, a nice companion (who might do us a favor once in a while). Someone to talk to and register our needs with. But when He comes in uninvited and disrupts our plans with songs of change? Our perspective shifts. It's surprising, inconvenient, and sometimes somewhat scary.

I tend to want to squash those uncomfortable thoughts. Things like loving my neighbor, my enemies, or the people who are diametrically opposed to me politically. The greedy and selfish, and those who have wronged me. It's one thing to be in church and nod in agreement to liturgy about "forgive the wrongs we have done, as we forgive the wrongs that others have done to us," you can repeat it while you're thinking about recipes; it's so rote and familiar. But it's another thing to have a face, a person, or a situation come unbidden to mind. Someone you know you ought to forgive and pray for.

God tucked away safely in a box? Comfortable, manageable. God disrupting my plans and asking me to step outside my comfort zone? Sometimes I want to squash those thoughts and requests like a bug. *No thanks.*

I don't know what songs of truth God is speaking to you, but recognize that it won't always be waterfalls and wonderment. Sometimes, it is. But sometimes, it's messy, uncomfortable, and demanding—but only if we resist.

I've never forgotten Katie Davis's story in her book about adopting African orphans, *Kisses From Katie*. She talks about the moment she realized that God wanted "*all* of her" not just Sunday Katie, or half-hearted Katie. He wants all of us too.

Like Little Miss Much Afraid in the book, *Hinds Feet on*

High Places, I balk at this more times than I'd like to admit. At one point my husband Tom asked me in exasperation, "Do you believe in all this or not?" My response to the particular situation was, "Yes, I do. *Theologically speaking.*"

Meaning, I see that it is true. I agree with God's Word. I know I should embrace it. But I'm finding it tough to do. My head knowledge isn't on the same level as my heart knowledge. My trust muscle is weak in some areas.

Tom responded, "You know, you are just a practicing Christian atheist when you talk that way, don't you?" *Ouch.* But yes, I suppose in some areas, I am. Like a person who claims they believe in the physics of flight but who is holding on to the plane wing while standing on the ground, they aren't going to fly.

❧ • ☙

When we mentally agree with what God says,
but don't do what He asks, we are
essentially practicing atheists.

❧ • ☙

Katie Davis addresses this fear we face when God's chirp is getting our attention, "We are not called to be safe, we are simply promised that when we are in danger, God is right there with us. And there is no better place to be than in His hands."

I have the erroneous notion that I can control God like a cricket. Keep Him in his cage, and have Him "sing" for me with lovely promises. But life and disruptions happen. World events and sickness happen. I can have the perspective that this is upsetting my plans, or I can perk up my ears. I don't know what the future holds, but He does. Maybe when I listen to His song, I'll find myself humming along and becoming a better me than I thought possible. And my fear and carefully wrought cages aren't protecting me; they are limiting me.

I hope in the dark, quiet moments, you hear the faint music of God. Or, in the middle of the hustle and bustle of Times Square, you hear His still, small voice. It might be alluring, mysterious, or scary. You might want to squash it, or tentatively welcome it. But He has promised that His call is a good thing. He says he delights in you. In Zephaniah 3:17, he states:

> "The Lord your God is with you, the Mighty Warrior who saves. He will take great delight in you; in his love he will no longer rebuke you, but will rejoice over you with singing."

Let this truth be foremost in your thoughts as you drift off tonight. The God of whispering trees, twinkling stars, shushing waves, and singing crickets rejoices over us with singing. Let's join in.

Moonlit Musings

1. Have you heard the still small voice of God calling to you in the night? Or in the middle of a busy moment? Do you tend to ignore that, or press in?
2. How have you "kept God in a cage"?
3. What verses or principles in the Bible make you uncomfortable? Why is that?
4. Have you ever felt like the author, that you believe

in things theologically and intellectually, but struggle to have those truths drop into your heart and change your choices?

Prayer

Heavenly Father,

All too often, I let the busyness of life drown out your sweet call to me. Help me slow down and spend time listening to you. Thank you that your Word says you delight in me! Help me discover your voice in your Word and obey it. Show me how to apply your truths to my daily life. And show me how to be the sweet chirp of hope to others who need to know you rejoice over them with singing.

In Jesus' name, amen.

[1] George Sheldon, The Cricket in Times Square (New York, Farrar, Straus and Giroux, 1960), 19.

CHAPTER 11

Scorpion

As a child, I was always filled with apprehension when we made our yearly sojourn to see relatives in Texas. Each spring, our family of five tumbled into my father's gigantic, green Lincoln Continental and made the interminable, bickering trip from Wisconsin to the Lone Star state.

My tension wasn't because I was stuck in the back seat with my two older siblings. It wasn't because I couldn't escape my parents' cigarette smoke. It wasn't because my father liked to see if he could drive 15 hours straight and make us hold our bladders until we thought we would burst. And it wasn't because we missed out on all the terribly exciting and promising sights along the way ("Dad! Look! The Jesse James hideout! Can we stop?").

No, my tension was because of all the stern warnings we got before we entered this foreign landscape.

"Don't ever let your sheets or bedding touch the floor!"

"Don't leave anything on the floor."

"Remember, always shake your shoes out before putting them on."

"Never go to the bathroom at night without a flashlight."

These were admonishments that we never heard in Wisconsin, or any other place we visited. This was because in Texas, there are scorpions, and they are most active at night.

Scorpions look like something Satan himself dreamed up as a pet. With their strange, lobster-on-land appearance, menacing front claws, and lethal tails arched up over their bodies—complete with a dagger stinger—they seemed poised to poison just by looking at them. You can almost hear them taunting like a Texan gunslinger, "You feeling lucky today pal? Wanna mess with me?" Heck no.

Although they look like over-sized insects or hard-shelled reptiles, they are, in fact, arachnids. They are part of the same family as spiders and ticks. They are also in a subgroup of arthropods called chelicerates. This makes them "cousins" to horseshoe crabs (another strange-looking character). But unlike spiders, ticks, and crabs, scorpions glow in UV light.

I discovered this years later when I ordered a black light (UV) flashlight. Our insecure male dog would decide to "mark" once in a while in our home. (Meaning, lift his leg and pee). I thought I was on top of the issue and washing up each infraction. But I smelled something. I could not find the source anywhere. While researching solutions, I read that these black lights show urine stains in a dark room, like a highlighter mark on a book page. And then, I watched the YouTube video of people using them for urine stains.

It was funny to watch this couple discovering areas that they hadn't realized their pets had defaced, the horror of bathroom walls after toilet-training their toddlers, but then they discovered an unexpected bonus. The black light revealed a glowing and sinister scorpion hiding under a piece of furniture.

There are about 2500 different kinds of scorpions in the world, and they live on every continent except Antarctica. The giant forest scorpion from India is the largest one in the world at about nine inches. In the United States, we have 90 species of scorpions, and Texas has 18 of them. The most common species in the Lone Star state is the striped bark scorpion. Adults are about 2 ½ inches long. Striped bark scorpions are yellowish-tan with two broad, dark stripes running the length of the back and have a dark triangular mark on the front of the head above the eyes.

Scorpions eat insects like spiders, so if you're an arachnophobe, I suppose that's a good thing. But they don't need to eat for months—and sometimes years—so I'm not so sure about benefits outweighing the danger.

Oddly, scorpions are choosy about their stings. Or rather, how much venom they release in their stings. They can decide just how much venom they discharge with each lash of their arched tails. They often kill prey with their front pincers if possible, resorting to venom only when threatened (like a foot coming down inside a shoe).

Although this venom can cause severe reactions

(nausea, vomiting, and rarely death), it can also serve a useful purpose. Scientists are uncovering more and more uses for scorpion toxins. A neuroscientist at the University of Alabama discovered that scorpion toxins would bind to glioma cells—aggressive brain cancer—and slow them down.

Scorpion venom has also been found to contain antimicrobial peptides that could be effective against bacteria, fungi, and malaria parasites. And arthritis sufferers might soon benefit from its anti-inflammatory properties. Other venom compounds have shown possibilities in the treatment of autoimmune disorders.

Although I probably wouldn't die from scorpion stings, my habit of walking outside barefoot was curtailed while in Texas. I learned down south to walk about with my head on a swivel. Rattlesnakes, tarantulas, and scorpions, oh my! I spent my yearly visits with a somewhat startled expression due to the constant barrage of sensory blasts.

So even though my Texan relatives had learned to coexist with rattlesnakes, copperheads, tarantulas, brown recluses, and scorpions, it still blew my mind when I learned about my great-aunt's bridge club.

One evening, my mother walked in on the ladies' monthly bridge meeting. This was in my great-aunt's beautiful, modern home. She had all-white furnishings and seamless, speckled terrazzo floors. She was a sculpture artist with impeccable taste. But this day, all the fashionable ladies sitting around the bridge table had their pedicured toes tucked up under them on the chairs. They sat there blowing Camel smoke, drinking cocktails, and playing bridge with scorpions skittering around under their chairs.

Seeing the surprised look on my mother's face, her aunt exhaled a plume of blue smoke between her Revlon-painted lips and drawled, "Honey, we just got plumb sick of watching out for these dang scorpions, so we just keep our feet up on the chairs. Watch yer step—there's several over yonder."

Apparently, there were more scorpions than usual that year, and they kept getting into her home. Rather than hysteria and stopping their card game, they just decided to draw their feet up and cope with it.

This laconic, Texan attitude to unusual circumstances was typical of my kinfolk. My great-aunt at 90 years old would kill rattlesnakes in her garden with a hoe. But I was astounded that these elegant women in this pristine home could be so casual and diffident about such a nasty threat right around and amongst them.

They just took it in stride. As if living amongst these threats was an everyday occurrence. Nothing to get excited about. And while it was startling to me as a young person, as I get older, this attitude makes more sense.

Every day, we witness new threats and learn to live with dangerous situations. It's happening so often, that what would have shocked us a decade ago we now take in stride.

Gang lootings in your favorite department store? No problem, order online.

Life-threatening heat waves? Just stay inside and turn up the air conditioning.

Random shootings at concerts and movie theaters? Avoid crowds and watch it on Netflix.

People brawling on planes and trying to open the door mid-flight? Just keep your eyes down, and don't get involved.

More and more we are becoming jaded to the startling, threatening situations around us. I barely notice when I see flags downtown at half-mast these days. Every day I expect a new shooting, a fresh tragedy. I've ceased wondering, "What happened? What world event made the flag be flown at half-mast today?" It has become business as usual. I'm losing any sense of shock and awe.

Some respond with looking back to golden-hued, halcyon days of the '50s when the economy was booming, moms stayed at home, children pledged allegiance, and there was a chicken in every pot. They think if we just rally enough and legislate enough, we can get back to the "good old days." But as my husband points out, those were the days where sin was just better hidden. Since time began, we've had violence, political upheaval, sex trafficking, and pedophilia. Today, it's just more exposed.

Instead of railing against the death of society and the apparent victories of the Visigoths, Huns, and vandals tearing down our cities and polluting neighborhoods, we've taken to shrugging our shoulders. Or at least tucking our feet up off the floor and getting on with life. But maybe, as followers of Christ, this is a good thing.

Because it so clearly demonstrates the fallacy of thinking: "Thanks to advances in technology, pharmacology and psychology, humans are just getting better and better and more advanced." No, we are not. We are selfish, hateful, greedy, violent, and all other adjectives that describe the situations listed above.

According to the Bible, this is business as usual.

"But mark this: There will be terrible times in the last days. People will be lovers of themselves, lovers of money, boastful, proud, abusive, disobedient to their parents, ungrateful, unholy, without love, unforgiving, slanderous, without self-control, brutal, not lovers of the good, treacherous, rash, conceited, lovers of pleasure rather than lovers of God—having a form of godliness but denying its power. Have nothing to do with such people" (2 Timothy 3:2-5).

That pretty much sums up today, doesn't it? This is our landscape, whether it feels foreign or not.

I can't help but wonder, if Jesus' believers honestly think and sing, "This world is not my home," why do we get so enraged when it's falling apart? He promised us that in this world we would have trouble. He said the world would hate us. What He never said was, "Lobby hard to get the Romans out of government. Stand up for and insist on your rights."

I'm not saying we shouldn't seek to rescue the perishing and innocents from destruction. But save yourself the shock, dismay, and rending of garments over it. This is life post-Eden.

After reading Matthew, Mark, Luke, and John, the only conclusion I can come to is this: Life is tough. Expect hardship. The Black Death, Pogroms, World Wars, pandemics, politics, and genocides have given us plenty of evidence of this. But Jesus said, in Him, we can find peace, order, and grace, no matter what chaos erupts around us. How do we get to that place of calm amidst such chaos?

For starters, I think we have to disabuse ourselves of the notion that life is only "good" when it's devoid of disappointment and hardship.

Katherine Wolf is an extraordinary example of this. This

gorgeous blonde was 26 years old, a happy newlywed with a new baby. And one day, without warning, she suffered a catastrophic stroke. She went through a sixteen-hour brain surgery, forty days in the ICU, a year in neurological rehab, and thirteen operations. Today, she lives with significant physical disabilities—but also joy. Their website (Hope-heals.com) reports:

> "They are dedicating their second-chance story to disrupting the myth that joy can only be found in a pain-free life. . .At first glance, Katherine and Jay's story seems exceptional. But the most personal stories are actually the most universal.

> "Who among us feels fully free, even when he can walk on his own? Who feels truly beautiful, even when her face is not paralyzed? Who feels completely understood, even without a speech impairment? The answer is a resounding "no one." We are all disabled. Some of our "wheelchairs" are simply on the inside instead of the outside.

> "If you have a pulse, you have problems and you have pain. But you also have a purpose that is simultaneously good and hard. When we choose to embrace the lives we're living this very day and release the lives we wished for, we can know in our deepest places that this good story is being written by a God who can't write any other kind of story. Living the good/hard life means we no longer need to numb ourselves to the difficult and the dark. We can awaken to the broken-down, miraculous nature of our second-chance lives and begin this very day to live them well to the very end.

> "At Hope Heals, our God-given, good/hard work is

to share what we've learned through a life we never imagined living: suffering is not the end of our story. It's the beginning of a new one. And we're writing our stories together."

I love that first sentence: "Disrupting the myth that joy can only be found in a pain-free life." We hear this message but don't really 'get it' until we are forced to 'live it.' Katherine and Jay Wolf are beacons to those who, when life smacks them around, wonder, where is God in all this? They help illuminate the way. You can read their story here: *www.hopeheals.com/who-we-are*.

Not all of us are dealing with catastrophic injuries. But we do deal with difficult people, demanding jobs, relationship breakdowns, physical infirmities, and just life's annoyances and problems. Plenty of things to rob us of the joy we hoped would infuse our lives as Jesus' followers.

I've noticed on the days I've wasted time doom-scrolling the news, feeling overwhelmed by the evil and craziness in the world, and realizing how little I can change things, the more I'm drawn to prayer. Complaining with friends, or doom-scrolling the YouTubers prepping for Armageddon doesn't accomplish the turning of the tide. It just keeps me focused on the darkness and despair, instead of on the light.

But turning our eyes off the blue light of our devices to the Light of the World can bring that peace Jesus promised.

There are several ways to do this. I usually first sigh and lift the situation or people up to God in prayer. I pray that people will come to their aid. I pray they would feel God's presence or whatever the situation calls for. I pray for the leaders of nations (even if I think they are utterly despicable). When I can't think of a single thing to pray about in a situation, I do what Jesus did. I say, "May your will be done on earth as it is in heaven." And then, I walk outside.

Once I stop paying homage to the urgency of the world's news and the evil that is skittering around us, I notice things lovely and sublime in creation. I focus on the birds, their songs, and their behaviors. I marvel at how different and colorful they are. I purposely focus on the various shapes of trees and the complexity and creativity of flowers. I notice children laughing at the beach, dogs joyfully running after balls, old folks walking arm in arm, owls hooting at dusk, and anything that reminds me that there is joy all around me and reasons to rejoice.

This might sound simplistic, but it's God's prescription for peace.

> "Rejoice in the Lord always. I will say it again: Rejoice! Let your gentleness be evident to all. The Lord is near. Do not be anxious about anything, but in every situation, by prayer and petition, with thanksgiving, present your requests to God. And the peace of God, which transcends all understanding, will guard your hearts and your minds in Christ Jesus. Finally, brothers and sisters, whatever is true, whatever is noble, whatever is right, whatever is pure, whatever is lovely, whatever is admirable—if anything is excellent or praiseworthy—think about such things. Whatever you have learned or received or heard from me, or seen in me—put it into practice. And the God of peace will be with you" (Philippians 4: 4-9).

Pay particular attention to those last two sentences: "Put it into practice and the God of peace will be with you." That is our prescription for peace amidst chaos.

*When we put His Word into practice,
we stop feeling hapless.*

The world really is on a downward spiral; you are not imagining it. But we don't have to wring our hands in despair. Peace can be found amidst it all.

Let's tuck our feet up and get on with life. Celebrate the good. Put God's Word into practice and the God of peace will be with you. This takes the sting out of life. This gives joy despite our circumstances.

And wear sturdy shoes.

Moonlit Musings

1. Have you ever met someone like my Texan great-aunties who are unperturbed by dangers and threats?
2. How do you usually react to threats—perceived or real?
3. Have you met anyone like Katherine Wolf, who finds joy despite harrowing hardship?
4. How can you practically, "Put it into practice" so that "the God of peace will be with you?" What would that look like for you? What steps would that entail?

Prayer

Heavenly Father,

This world seems just out of control at times. It's so reassuring that you are not surprised or perplexed. It's amazing that in the 1st century, they could describe so perfectly what our world looks like today. Thank you for Your Word which reminds me to "not be anxious about anything." You are the Alpha and the Omega, you know the beginning and the end.

In Jesus' name, Amen.

CHAPTER 12

Skunk

S tars were winking in the sky when I got off work and made it to my sister's house for dinner. I threaded the path from the driveway to her back door. There were no lights to guide my feet, but I knew the way. The resident owls were hooting in the distance, and I was imagining the warm welcome I would get from my little nephews. Rounding the corner of the house, I saw her two cats milling about. Silhouetted by the light from the back door, I could see their big, fluffy tails held up high.

"Kitties!" I greeted them. Dropping my heavy tote bag, I leaned into the light to give them a pet. But I snatched my hand away and jerked back in horror. These "kitties" had a white stripe down the center of their backs! They weren't kitties at all. They were skunks scrounging around for cat kibble and bird seed scattered by the door.

Maybe they were too busy looking for food, but they didn't pay me much attention as I performed an impromptu, backward, shuffling moonwalk for another entry point.

Anytime I've chanced upon a skunk, I've marveled at their nonchalance. They aren't all that fussed about me intruding in their space. They don't have to act aggressive and threatening because they know they have the ultimate weapon. Very few predators bother with skunks. Or if they do, it's as my husband would say after an unpleasant moment, "Well, that was a once-in-a-lifetime moment!" (As in, never going to this restaurant again, thank you very much!) Only the supremely foolish or ignorant animal messes with a skunk.

But there is one animal that seeks out skunks regularly as prey. This animal apparently doesn't sense the stench and isn't affected by it. In fact, he considers skunk a delicious meal. Silently swooping down from the velvet skies to nab a skunk is the Great Horned Owl. Since this owl can carry prey equal to his body weight—unlike other owls—this is an easy, fast-food meal for him. One Great Horned Owl's nest was found with the remains of 57 skunks. Clearly, this is a favorite food! And there is no way Mr. Skunk has any premonition to know if he is coming. Owl feathers are designed so that their flight is silent. While skunks have a good sense of smell and hearing, their eyesight is poor. They can't see much past 10 feet. (This poor eyesight, plus they can't run very fast, is why they often end up as roadkill.) The owl, on the other hand, has superb night vision. The only danger to our owl from the skunk is if he gets sprayed in the eyes and becomes blinded. A blind owl is a starving and soon dead owl. Wildlife refuges frequently take in owls with eye injuries and smelling of skunk.

So, how do skunks release this pungent aroma? How much do they store in their bodies? And how often can they spray it—do they ever run out?

Skunks have two glands on the sides of their anus that release the oil-based spray with little jets—or nipples—that they can control with muscles to aim them. Before spraying, a skunk will warn you with hisses and foot-stamping before turning his back end towards you. Then, they can hit their target with great accuracy up to 15 feet away. The spotted skunk (similar to the striped skunk but with broken white lines) will do a handstand with his head looking backward through his arms, his face and bottom both aimed toward the target while spraying.

While the aroma is enough to cause burning, streaming eyes, and vomiting, it's a surprisingly small amount. They only carry about a tablespoon of the odoriferous oil. But they can spray this atomized concoction in bursts of five times in a row. Then, it takes about a week to replenish the supply.

Contrary to popular thought, tomato juice is not the best way to wash off this oil. American chemist Paul Krebaum developed a recipe that chemically neutralizes skunk spray by changing the chemicals that cause the smell into odorless acids. His recipe is 1 quart of 3% hydrogen peroxide, ¼ cup of baking soda, and 1-2 teaspoons of liquid dish soap. (I would say use Dawn™ dish soap—it is superior in getting rid of oils.) The Humane Society of the United States recommends this recipe for washing pets and clothing. Warning: Do not try to store this mixture; it can burst the container.

Even if skunks aren't spraying near your house, if you have them nearby (or under your house), the odor is inescapable. How do you get rid of them? The worst thing you can do is poison them. Now you have a rotting, skunk-smelling mess on your hands. Plus, you've also probably killed a few owls since they feed upon them.

Skunks are deterred by strong smells such as Vicks VapoRub™ or ammonia. Closing off entry points under your home and spreading these smells around will do much to deter them. Also, keeping a lantern lit where they like it to be dark also deters them. I would consider installing a few owl nesting boxes on nearby trees. You get to hear the romantic hooting at night after they've killed and eaten your unwelcome visitors.

Usually, you can smell skunks before you see them. Whether you're driving down a road on a summer night or you live in an area where they like to roam, the scent of skunk is distinctive, pungent, and clinging. It's so strong that often my husband and I get awakened in the middle of the night due to Pepe LePew roaming by. His scent is so pervasive it wafts through our screens 20 feet above the walkway and into our bedroom windows, somewhat gagging us. Studies have shown that skunk smell can be detected a mile away from the source, so even if you don't see them, you can smell them.

Skunks aren't the only mammals with a distinctive odor. Badgers and wolverines can also excrete an offensive stench that isn't as strong as a skunk's but is still pretty repellent. Humans also carry a distinctive scent.

Ask any hunter why they pay attention to which way the wind is blowing. They'll tell you that no matter how they bathe or saturate themselves in other odors, if they are upwind from their prey, the prey will smell their scent and it will scare off the animal.

I first noticed in college that different people had different, distinctive smells. When you walk into someone's dormitory room, you smell their bedding, clothes, and unique scent. Any mother of teenage boys will tell you they notice a new, particular odor once their boys enter puberty. Some relationship experts will say we are attracted or repelled by others partly because of their scent. And the Bible confirms this.

In the book of 2 Corinthians, the apostle Paul describes a Roman military triumph:

> "But thanks be to God, who always leads us in triumph in Christ, and manifests through us the sweet aroma of the knowledge of Him in every place. For we are a fragrance of Christ to God among those who are being saved and among those who are perishing; to the one an aroma from death to death; to the other, an aroma from life to life" (2 Corinthians 2:14-16 NASB).

What Paul is describing here is a victory parade. When the Roman army defeated an enemy, there would be a grand parade—or triumphant procession. First in the parade lineup would be the vanquished captives in chains, destined for death. Then would come the spoils of war—gold, silver, armor, and statues. Next would be the Roman senators and officials, and after them, the general's bodyguards. Following them would be the purple-robed general wearing a laurel wreath, riding on a chariot. Everywhere, all along the triumphant route of the procession would be strewn flowers and the smell of incense from burning altars would fill the air.

To the conquerors, the aroma of incense would signify victory and celebration. To the captured in chains, it was the smell of death because once the procession had completed its route, the captured were immediately put to death. So, Paul is saying that living out our lives as followers of Jesus will cause an aroma to emanate from us. To one group, it will be repugnant, a smell of loss and death. To another, His victory over sin, death, and new life for believers will be the aroma of triumph and joy.

It's wild when you see this play out in your own life. In my book *This Outside Life*, I wrote about a time when my aroma of Christ hit someone like the stench of skunk. Mind you, I wasn't preaching or anything; I was just living my life. But the odor pervaded, apparently.

I was working in San Francisco at my first job out of college. A group of women had gone out to lunch to discuss an upcoming ski trip we were planning. Suddenly, without provocation, one of the women looked at me with a sneer and said, "Are you going to bring any of your goody-goody church ladies along?" I was stunned. I had never discussed my faith life with her, so how could she know I was in a Bible study group?

And furthermore, among the "church ladies" were survivors of sex addiction, incest, and drug abuse. So, not exactly a goody-goody group either. Everyone at the table was openmouthed at her attack until someone else tactfully changed the subject.

For days afterward, I couldn't figure out the *why* of that comment. Why did she say that? Why did it matter to her whether or not I was in a Bible study group after work? (Did she think it would affect my skiing?) Why had she felt the need to embarrass and attack me like that?

Later, I learned that her grandmother had been murdered in a random shooting while coming home from errands. She was bitter and angry with God for allowing such a horrific event to devastate her family. To her, anything to do with God was a stench in her nostrils. It made sense to me, and I understood that she wasn't angry with me per se, but with who I represented.

We can't know everyone's background or spiritual journey, so it's pointless to overthink how our aroma affects others. It's between them and God to work out their frustrations and failures. Although we would like to be "the sweet aroma of the knowledge of Him in every place," we can't control others' reactions. But know this: as a follower of Jesus, you have an aroma, and not everyone will welcome it.

To be around Jesus was to inhale the fragrance of life in its fullness. Jesus exuded a pleasing aroma when He turned water into wine at a wedding party so the host wouldn't be embarrassed. To His mother, who made the request, and to the party's host, it was the aroma of compassion. When He called the shunned tax collector Zacchaeus out of the tree and offered to have dinner with him, He was the aroma of inclusion. When He healed the leper, the blind, and the crippled, He was the aroma of mercy. When He cried at the death of Lazarus, He was the aroma of empathy. When He hung out with sinners, He was the aroma of fellowship. When Jesus hung on the cross—beaten, bloodied, and innocent—He was the aroma of love. After the resurrection, when He gave Peter the responsibility to "feed my lambs" despite Peter denying Him, He was the aroma of forgiveness.

When we follow in Jesus's footsteps and show compassion, inclusion, mercy, empathy, fellowship, love, and forgiveness, we are a "sweet aroma of the knowledge of Him in every place." That fragrance can be so compelling; it either draws people and changes lives or repels them. Even when it doesn't make sense, we can make perfect 'scents.'

❧ • ❦

When we pour our lives out for others,
even when it doesn't make sense,
we can make perfect scents.

❧ • ❦

The disciples didn't think it made sense when a woman came in while He was having dinner at Simon the Leper's home, broke open an alabaster jar of expensive perfume, and poured it over Jesus's head. As the valuable nard dripped through His hair and the scent wafted through the room, the disciples indignantly protested that it was a great waste of resources. She could have sold that for a year's wages. Jesus had a different reaction.

> "Leave her alone," said Jesus, "Why are you bothering her? She has done a beautiful thing to me. The poor you will always have with you, and you can help them any time you want. But you will not always have me. She did what she could. She poured perfume on my body beforehand to prepare for my burial. Truly I tell you, wherever the gospel is preached throughout the world, what she has done will also be told, in memory of her" (Mark 14:6-9).

When we pour ourselves out as a fragrant offering in love and service to others, we leave a sweet, lasting memory of the pleasing aroma of Christ. And that's a scent to die for.

Moonlit Musings

1. Are there any smells or scents you just can't stand?
2. Have you had anyone react to you in a strange, negative way when you didn't say or do anything to provoke them? Why do you think that was?
3. Which aroma of Christ do you find most alluring; compassion, inclusion, mercy, empathy, fellowship, love, or forgiveness?
4. Jesus was touched by the prostitute's demonstration of gratitude for what He had done for her. How could you be a little extravagant in your appreciation for Him?

Prayer

Heavenly Father,

Too often, I think more about how I look—or appear—to others than representing you. I don't think about my reactions or presence in terms of scent. Please show me how to exhibit your aroma of compassion, mercy, and forgiveness to others. Help me be the "sweet aroma of the knowledge of you in every place." And bring to mind ways I can be extravagant in demonstrating my gratitude to you.

In Jesus' name, amen.

Nature at Night

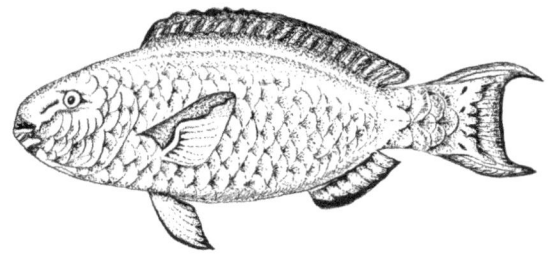

CHAPTER 13

Parrot Fish

I waited at the entrance to the cave, its vast, inky darkness yawning wide before me. My breath escaped my regulator in silvery bubbles that caught the moonlight and shimmered to the water's surface. Although it was calm in the water that night, my heart wasn't calm. I wasn't going into that cave. *No way.*

My dive buddy had other plans. He thought nothing about swimming into a cave on a night dive. Wasn't it scary enough out here? Wasn't it enough to shine our flashlights on coral and watch the Christmas tree worms fold up and disappear? Wasn't there enough out here in this black nothingness to challenge our courage? And what about being my dive "buddy?" We were supposed to stick together. That's a diving rule you don't break.

I exhaled a rush of frustrated bubbles and began to look around. A few of my bubbles caught under something and caused it to sway towards the entrance. What was that?

It looked like a fish caught in a butterfly cocoon; its bright colors muted by the white, gauzy bubble that surrounded it. Was it dead? I peered closer. Its protruding beak-like mouth and front teeth, combined with riotous fuchsia and turquoise colors, identified it as one of my favorites—a parrot fish!

I enjoy watching these carnival-colored fish munching on the coral during snorkeling on day dives. If you get close enough, you can even hear the loud crunching as they munch through chunks of coral. The parrot fish's teeth are fused as one to their jawbone, and their munching power is so strong that their bite strength is 530 tons of pressure per square inch (psi). A great white shark's bite strength is 625 psi. So not a huge difference. Kind of remarkable for a soft, pretty fish you think would look nice in your aquarium.

Parrot fish eat the coral for the algae, and getting rid of algae is beneficial to the reef. And all this crunching and munching produces a lot of sand—some estimates put it at approximately up to 90 kilograms (or 198 pounds) of sand each year per fish. Another estimate I read said it was more like 1000 pounds—the weight of a baby grand piano. Either way, if you swim behind a parrot fish, you will see the little trail of digested coral leave its body in a nearly continuous stream of fine grains. It is the reef's quirky and colorful sand machine.

I was already a fan of this unique and colorful fish, but why was he in this bubble? I could see the eyes move and gills and fins slowly moving. So, it was alive! But why in this weird, white film that encapsulated it? My fishy friend swayed in the current of the water. I slowly gazed at it from different angles. Did a predator wrap him up for a future meal? Like spiders do with their prey in webs? I backed up and glanced around for the giant eel, which I was sure would loom out and swallow my face. Nobody home. Just me and my parrot fish friend in his gauzy, watery, sleeping bag.

Eventually, my dive buddy appeared from the depths of his cave exploration, and we continued investigating the ocean at night. But I couldn't wait to surface and find out about my companion at the cave entrance.

Whether you prefer flannel or crisp cotton sheets, down comforters, or grandma's quilt, we all have a favorite way to wrap ourselves for sleep each night. And the parrot fish does too. The eerie, milky "sleeping bag" I saw around this colorful fish is what he prefers to sleep in. But unlike our sheets and blankets, his is made of mucus.

Every night, while the cleaner shrimp scatter off to sleep and avoid predators, the parrot fish makes this mucus bubble to protect itself from parasites and predators. It's somewhat like our version of mosquito netting. Glands in the parrot fish's gills secrete the mucus, which slowly comes out of the fish's mouth until it completely encases him. This process takes about an hour. Scientists think this mucus cocoon might also help mask his scent from predators like moray eels and sharks.

In times of doubt, stress or anxious thoughts, I too create a cocoon like this to protect me from marauding thoughts and parasitic beliefs that prevent my sleep. My mother started this for me when I was little. When I would tell her of my nighttime fears she would wave her hands over me and say, "Oh, don't worry! There is an invisible shield of protection around you!"

But my mother isn't around anymore, and if we're healthy adults, we shouldn't be sleeping with the aid of our mothers. So, what's an anxious heart to do?

Fear, anxious thoughts, imagined threats, and sleepless nights are nothing new to biblical writers. And for that, I'm so thankful. They, too, understand heart-pounding scenarios racing through our heads. They too, have wet their pillow with tears. They, too, are human like we are.

They use words like, "My God, my God, why have you forsaken me? Why are you so far from saving me, so far from my cries of anguish?" (Psalm 22:1). And, "I am worn out from my groaning. All night long I flood my bed with weeping and drench my couch with tears" (Psalm 6:6).

I have been there. Many times. Whether I'm worried about the economy, jobs, my family members, rising crime in our neighborhood, or just the scary state of the world, there's no shortage of night terrors to keep me tossing and turning. One night stands out in particular.

It was a few years after the 2008 everything crash, and our house had been on the market for about a year. No buyers. And we were churning through our savings like hot dogs at an eating contest. I lay in bed and stared at the ceiling while my husband snored peacefully beside me. What was going to happen to us? What if we ran through our savings, then what? What if we had medical issues and couldn't pay? What if? What if? Tears slipped down the sides of my face and ran into my ears. The lyrics of the song we had sung in church that morning were running through my mind, "The name of the Lord is a strong tower…" *Humpf!* I thought, with growing bitterness, *a fat lot of good that was doing me now!* I swung my legs over the side and got up, tired of staring at the ceiling and tired of all the scenarios playing through my head.

I softly padded down to the room where our bookcases were and scanned the titles. Anything. Something. I needed some sort of elixir to give me courage and help me sleep. I saw a biography my mother-in-law had given me and pulled it out. I was aware of this author's story. As a missionary, she had been caught up in the events of WW2 and became a Japanese prisoner of war in Papua, New Guinea. Horrific events like beatings, rats nibbling on toes, and starvation were part of her story. "Well, if she can live through that, I can probably find some courage here," I thought. I flipped through the pages, and my eyes fell on these words written while she was in a jail cell:

"Gradually I drifted into the spiritually unprofitable game of "suppose"! *Suppose* the Japanese do win the war, what then?. . . *Suppose* none of us makes it home?

"There is nothing that will plunge a person into despair more quickly than to suppose what could happen. This was another example of the worries of tomorrow that never come, robbing us of the joys of today. . .

"O Lord," I cried, "forgive me. It isn't a game of 'suppose.' I live in the sure knowledge that "the name of the Lord is a strong tower: the righteous runneth into it, and is safe" (Proverbs 18:10). The name of Jesus, Your precious name is my strong tower of defense against the enemy of despair. It is my shelter that is secure; I enter in and am safe."[1]

My jaw dropped, and tears began to flow down my face. What were the odds that this scenario, from a woman in a prison cell 60 years ago, would refer to this verse, that was the exact verse in the song that I couldn't get out of my head, on this night when I needed it most? I stood in quiet awe in the magnitude of the moment.

Clearly, God had just thrown me my own protective parrot fish bubble to wrap myself in for the night.

With the sure certainty of God knowing what I was going through, of Him carefully orchestrating the circumstances of me finding that page and speaking to me through the scriptures, my heart was completely altered. I felt joy and hope surging through me. Confident that the God of the universe who set the galaxies spinning cared enough to reach down and settle my spinning heart.

I didn't have any solutions, but I did have surety. He knows. He cares.

❧•☙

When we search for distractions and stare at our phone's pictures, we're missing out on the solace of His scriptures.

❧•☙

While obviously, this sort of heaven-sent assurance doesn't happen most nights, it's okay because I don't need it. What I need is to stop looking for solace in my screens. What I need is to refuse refuge in the refrigerator. What I need is to remind myself of the truth. I can wrap myself in the protective love of God and His promises to never leave me.

"Be strong and courageous. Do not be afraid or terrified because of them, for the LORD your God goes with you; he will never leave you nor forsake you" (Deuteronomy 31: 6-7).

I can choose to remember He will always love me. "The LORD appeared to us in the past, saying: 'I have loved you with an everlasting love; I have drawn you with unfailing kindness'" (Jeremiah 31:3).

I can wrap myself in the sure knowledge of his promise to watch over me.

> "I will lift up my eyes to the mountains;
>   From where shall my help come?
> My help comes from the LORD
>   Who made heaven and earth.
> He will not allow your foot to slip;
>   He who keeps you will not slumber.
> Behold, He who keeps Israel
>   Will neither slumber nor sleep.
> The LORD is your keeper;
>   The LORD is your shade on your right hand.
> The sun will not smite you by day,
>   Nor the moon by night.
> The LORD will protect you from all evil;
>   He will keep your soul.
> The LORD will guard your going out and
>   your coming in
> From this time forth and forever" (Psalm
>   121 NASB).

When the parasitic thoughts of doubt and fear start nibbling on my heart, I create my own cocoon of protection. I recite verses to myself that talk about God's provision and protection. And then I drift, peacefully bobbing in the currents of truth and love that I have wrapped around my heart and mind.

Every night, the parrot fish makes its mucus cocoon of protection. Every night, so can we.

Moonlit Musings

1. What topics have kept you tossing and turning in thoughts of "what if" and "suppose?"
2. Have you ever had the experience where a snippet from a song, or a scripture has been running through your mind, and then you encounter the exact same message from another source?
3. What distractions or self-soothing do you resort to when you are anxious? Games? Food? Drink? Binge watching shows?
4. Which of these verses, Deuteronomy 31:6-7, Jeremiah 31:3, or Psalm 121 brings you the most comfort?

Prayer

Heavenly Father,

Thank you for the surety of your Word, which reminds me of your care and love. I am so grateful that David wrote Psalms about how he wet his pillow with tears. I can relate to that. And yet, he was confident of your steadfast love and protection. Please help me to memorize some of your verses of provision to wrap my mind in at night.

In Jesus' name, amen.

[1] From Evidence Not Seen by Darlene Deibler Rose, copyright 1988, 1990.

CHAPTER 14

Beaver

With his nose buried in a pile of laundry, the beaver pushed his load down the hallway in the home. His characteristic, flat, pancake tail dragged behind him. Next, he grabbed the doormat with his delicate, long-fingered paws and pulled that down the hallway. It could be anything: dolls, laundry, scatter rugs, whatever he could grab and drag. Whatever he could get his "hands" on, he pushed, nudged, and commandeered for his dam creation. He just couldn't help himself. It was what he was made to do.

Beavers are extraordinarily good at making dams. There are several reasons for this. Although they are our biggest rodent (weighing in at around 40 – 60 pounds), it's not their size that makes them so skilled. They have a set of transparent eyelids that cover their eyes as they swim. Their lips close behind their teeth, which allows them to bite down on a branch, swim underwater, and not drown. They can stay underwater for 15 minutes. And their dense, thick, oily fur keeps them warm even when lakes freeze over.

Then there is that tail. The long, broad, flat beaver tail is about 12–15 inches long, 6 inches wide, and 2 inches thick. Contrary to popular myth, they do not use it like a trowel for plastering when building their mud and stick dams. Covered with leathery scales and sparse hair, the tail is an area for storing fat and regulating heat. When he's gnawing down branches or dragging them into the water, the tail serves as a counterbalance and support. While in the water, the tail acts as a rudder. It's also an alarm system.

My father told me of a night spent camping around lakes in northern Minnesota when he was a boy. He was with his father (a tall, thoughtful Norwegian who had emigrated at seventeen with fifteen dollars in his pocket). They had just settled down for the night when a noise like gunshots caused my father to bolt upright. Was someone shooting guns in the night? Were they in danger? My grandfather reassured him, "It's only beavers, son, settle down."

Beavers slap their tails on the water as a warning system when they want to warn family members about predators or encourage competitive suitors to turn away. Apparently, on a quiet summer night, the sound carries over the water like a gunshot.

I wonder now how my grandfather knew so much about beavers. He came to America from Norway when he was a teenager. By then, most of the beavers had been wiped out in Europe from the atavistic desire for beaver pelts in the 1700s and 1800s. This culling of beavers also happened in North America (reducing the population from 100–200 million to a few thousand). However, reintroduction efforts have been successful both here and, to a smaller extent, in France, Germany, Poland, Scandinavia, and Russia.

Not everyone is thrilled about the beavers' reintroduction. Some argue that they ruin the landscape, introduce flooding, and are generally a nuisance. Scientists who study the flow of water (hydrologists) say that the beaver dams act as a necessary "speed bump" for water flows. The dams are a little leaky, which slows the flow of water and creates valuable wetlands. These wetlands allow microorganisms to detoxify pesticides, prevent algae blooms, and provide habitat for frogs, salamanders, fish, birds, and other mammals. This makes a quiet nursery for natural fisheries to thrive. They also filter out silt so that the downstream water is even clearer. One estimate says that nearly half of all endangered and threatened species need wetlands to survive. And it's for that reason—and the beavers' dams—they are called a "keystone species."

One study analyzing the importance of beaver dams in Rocky Mountain National Park discovered that the dams raised the water table, which caused water to spread through the valley. This helped it stay moist even during dry seasons. Having beaver dams in the headwaters of rivers reduces the flow and keeps water on the land longer, thereby reducing the severe impact of droughts, something significant in these days of increasing heat and dry spells.

But our housebound beaver we met at the beginning of

this chapter wasn't out in the wild, creating valuable wetlands. Why was he so obsessed with making dams?

It turns out that JB (Justin Beaver) was orphaned as a baby (or "kit," as baby beavers are called). So, for the time being, he was being fostered in a home until they could rehabilitate him into the wild. The foster mom posted videos showing JB doing what beavers do: grab, drag, and dam (and chew through furniture legs). But something struck me about this sweet little mammal famous for his cutting teeth and dam-building capabilities. He never had this modeled for him.

JB was so young when he was rescued that he didn't get any "training" from his mother. Nobody showed him how to build a dam. Nobody showed him how to gnaw on wood. Nobody demonstrated to him that this is what beavers do. He just had it hard-wired in him.

Just as animals can be hard-wired for specific talents and behaviors, I believe God hard-wires gifts and talents into all of us. And when we try to do or be someone else, we invite misery and frustration into our lives.

I thought about the years I had wasted trying to be more organized in certain areas of my life. My good friend, Lynne, is a British quintessential Mary Poppins—practically perfect in every way. She teaches preschoolers. She is always immaculately put together. She is extremely organized, whether it's a closet, her schedule, or her vacations. Her photo albums are up to date. Her home is always "tour ready." In short, she is the opposite of me.

And the message I've been telling myself is, "I need to be more like Lynne." The thoughts go like this; "You need to be more organized! See how smoothly her life runs? If you were more like her, you'd get more done. You'd have less chaos. Everything in your life would be better." The result? I ignore the talents that God gave me (creativity, writing, painting, spontaneity, etc.) I try to become someone with skills that are not native to my design.

It takes about 150% of my thoughts and efforts to run my life like Lynne's. It totally exhausts me. For her? It's just everyday life. She doesn't give it much thought. So, what happens when I spend all that time and effort trying to exhibit her natural talents? I cause myself a lot of frustration and wasted time, and I don't accomplish the things that I do well. I don't write. I don't paint. I don't dream up projects. I don't produce podcasts. I don't do creative me. The way God made me.

My husband will tell you that he can determine whether I'm operating within my God-given talents or not. When I'm being me, there's a smile on my face. There's a bounce to my step. I'm brimming over with thousands of creative ideas. The world seems bright, positive, and full of possibilities. When I'm trying to be someone else? I have a frown. I find fault with family members. I'm disgruntled quickly. I overeat. I feel self-loathing. I am Not Fun to be around. He prefers the God-made me. Not the I-ought-to-be-me persona.

When we operate within our talents and God-directed design, life runs a bit smoother. It's not so much a struggle as it is fun—sometimes even a joy. Some call it being "in the flow."

Focusing most of our attention and energy on areas that we are not strong in is a fool's errand. It takes an enormous toll on our energy and sanity. It drains our enthusiasm for life, clouds our vision, and makes us feel like defeated losers.

I first learned this foolishness when I read a business book about operating within your strengths. The author proposed that focusing most of our time on areas we are weak in is a waste of time. We should double down on what we do well. That's where we excel. That's where we would see the most significant improvement in our lives. We could attempt to shore up our weak areas (or, better yet, hire out those projects). Still, if we really want to make a difference, we need to zero in on our areas of genius and our talents and go with the flow.

Since I've appropriated this outlook, I spend less time beating myself up that I'm not more like Lynne. While I admire her (and often get tips from her), there is no way I will ever be as organized as she is. That's not how God hard-wired or designed me. He made me with different talents. I've learned to let go of the foolish notion that I "ought" to be more like her.

My sister manages hundreds of people. It's easy for her. The thought of doing that makes me nauseous. I would worry too much that everyone was happy and liked me. I couldn't imagine organizing all that. But for her, it's operating the way God wired her. She enjoys it. I'd rather run down the street naked.

You can see this in some children at an early age. My brother-in-law lost my niece in Chicago's O'Hare airport when she was four years old. This is one of the busiest airports in the world. At that age, I would have been sobbing, curled up in a corner, completely freaking out, and probably wetting my pants. My niece? She marched her little self up to a ticket agent and declared, "You need to make an announcement and find my dad, *he's lost.*" This incident speaks volumes about who she is at her core. And she has always been like this. To this day, she could rule the world with a plan if given the reins. She is in charge and knows what to do.

As parents, we like to think we can mold and shape our kids. Good luck with that. I mean, if you've been a student of your child and studied their gifts, talents, and preferences, you soon see that you can't force a sensitive musician to become an All-American rugby player. They enter this world with a particular bent, and we can help encourage these talents to bear fruit like a pruned and trained fruit tree or waste our time forcing them into a mold we want for them.

The Bible has a verse for this. "Train up a child in the way he should go, and when he is old he will not depart from it" (Proverbs 22:6 NKJV). Most think this means if you threaten, spank, and make them memorize verses, you will turn out a God-fearing proper citizen. I think you'll turn out an embittered, resentful teenager who doesn't want your God.

This verse has more of a flavor of training a fruit tree. How much better it is to encourage what it was made to do already? I like how the Bible paraphrased version, *The Message*, puts it: "Point your kids in the right direction— when they are old they won't be lost."

We got our son LEGO robotics because that was his passion. While I tried to encourage him to draw and paint, it wasn't his jam. Under my coaching, he produced nice work, but he really excelled in the areas of science, math, and music endeavors. He is not overly loud and gregarious like most of my family of origin. He prefers a few people and quiet demonstrations of subdued emotion. I had to learn to decipher this because it was different from my bent or language.

We can persist in the frustrating task of forcing kids into our plans or encourage them to walk into a liberating path of their God-given gifts and talents. Or, as a 12-step person once asked me, "How much pain do you want?"

Exodus chapter 35 is a clarion call to people who feel God made a mistake either with their kids or themselves. Here we see Moses telling the people that God purposely instills specific gifts and abilities in us.

> Then Moses said to the Israelites, "See, the Lord has chosen Bezalel son of Uri, the son of Hur, of the tribe of Judah, and he has filled him with the Spirit of God, with wisdom, with understanding, with knowledge and with all kinds of skills—to make artistic designs for work in gold, silver and bronze, to cut and set stones, to work in wood and to engage in all kinds of artistic crafts. And he has given both him and Oholiab son of Ahisamak, of the tribe of Dan, the ability to teach others. He has filled them with skill to do all kinds of work as engravers, designers, embroiderers in blue, purple and scarlet yarn and fine linen, and weavers—all of them skilled workers and designers" (Exodus 35:30-35).

Did you notice the detail in the above verses? God specifically instilled various skills and talents in these people. Talent to work with wood, cut stones, metal working, weaving, designing, and teaching others. Can you imagine the folly of Moses saying something like, "Nah! I think they should be hunters or cooks. That's what our family likes to do."

⁂

We can persist in the frustrating task of forcing kids into our plans or encourage them to walk into a liberating path of their God-given gifts and talents.

⁂

It does our kids a crushing disservice to communicate something is "wrong" with them because they are not like us. They are how God meant them to be; our job is to encourage those gifts and talents. You're on the highway to heartbreak if you try to force them down other paths. They will excel when they operate within their natural bent—*the way they should go.*

Beavers are cute, good for the environment, and excel in dam building. But as house pets? Not if you value your furniture. Guard animals? No way. Pack animals? Never. Their Creator gifted them with the ability to build dams and live a particular life, which they are extraordinarily skilled to do. So are you.

Moonlit Musings

1. What skills or talents do you have and think are no big deal, but others have commented on?
2. What activities bring you the most peace, contentment, or joy while doing? This doesn't have to be

artistic; it could be organizing closets or running a company.

3. Have you ever wasted time trying to be like someone else?

4. What weak areas of your life could you get others to do? Or hire it done?

Prayer

Father God,

You are amazingly creative and excellent in all you have made. Thank you for all the artists, tradesmen, athletes, executives and skilled people you have endowed with talents and abilities. Thank you for the abilities you have given me! Please help me grow in my talents and serve others with them. Help me show appreciation for the specific ways you have created my family members, coworkers, and others I come across in my daily life. They are all representations of your glory, and they are to be celebrated.

In Jesus' name, amen.

CHAPTER 15

Hare

Y ou need to come by and see my meadow," my sister said. "It's really coming into its own right now." Since she is a prolific gardener with many acres under her trowel and tutelage, I suspected this might be worth going out of my way for.

I often get these invitations from her. "The wisteria is unbelievable right now! You've got to come by and see it draped all around the fountain." Or, "If you don't come before the rain later this week, you'll miss the roses at their best—particularly those climbers. This is their first flush." Although she only lives 18 miles away, busy schedules constantly delay my visits, and I don't always get there in time for the glorious appearance of her flora.

But a "meadow" sounded enchanting—something you only see in pictures of the Cotswolds in England or a rare spot dotted with wild lupines and tucked between mountains, fed by a stream. I knew she had planned and seeded this lot of land carefully, and I was curious to see her results.

At five o'clock, the sun had dropped behind the tall evergreens surrounding the meadow when I opened the gate. It closed behind me with a soft, metallic *snick*. The lack of direct sunlight made the air softened, diffused, and quieter. A deepening cobalt blue filled the sky as my feet crunched along the gravel path. Bluebirds swooped on the meadow edges, snapping up the day's last insects, and a mockingbird called from the trees. I strolled down the path and marveled at the thigh-high daisies, blue bachelor buttons, fairy-pink gaura, and bright red poppies brushing my fingertips. Fat, lazy bees floated around the wild grasses, and gorgeous colors undulated in the breeze, totally beguiling me.

Lost in my reverie, I was utterly unprepared for the explosion of fur across the path in front of me. A large, brown animal bolted up from behind a clump of pink godetia and white daisies and made a 10-foot leap across the path. He zigzagged twice, and I caught a glimpse of two incongruously long ears. His surprisingly large size, huge back legs, and enormous ears helped me identify him. This must be my sister's resident jackrabbit she told me about.

Although I had heard he lived here, I was startled by his size. Much bigger than the sweet rabbits that scooted out of the way with half-hearted hops, this guy was altogether different. In fact, jackrabbits are not rabbits at all; they are *hares*.

In the United States, we have 3 kinds of hares. The blacktail jackrabbit (*Lepus californicus*), the whitetail jackrabbit

(*L. townsendii*), and the snowshoe hare (*L. americanus*). Also in limited areas are the antelope jackrabbit (*L. alleni*) and the European hare (*L. europaeus*). While most people use the terms jackrabbit, hare, and rabbit interchangeably, they are not the same. The jackrabbit—or hare—is much larger and faster.

A rabbit or bunny is a cute, round mammal with shorter ears, big eyes, and a docile temperament. Peter Rabbit, that cute fluffy character from Beatrix Potter's books, is a rabbit. Peter Cottontail (often confused with Peter Rabbit) is the character in Gene Autry's popular 1950 Easter song, is also a rabbit. Rabbits are social, living underground in colonies and warrens—or burrows. Hares raise their young above ground, and their young are born fully furred, eyes open, and able to move about at birth. The rabbit is born naked, blind, and entirely dependent.

Although both rabbits and hares are from the family *Leporidae*, the jackrabbit is the bigger, faster, monster-truck version. Jackrabbits were so named because when the first settlers came West across the prairies and they spied the enormous ears of the hares, they were reminded of the long ears of a jackass (male donkey). And so, they called them jackrabbits.

Its size is the most visually noticeable difference between a hare and a rabbit. Rabbits are much smaller than hares, measuring about 15" long and weighing around 4 pounds. In comparison, hares can reach up to 28"—over 2 feet— and weigh about 11 pounds fully grown. And while the rabbit has a rounded, adorable face, the hare has a longer and more angular head, almost like a horse. And the hare's oversized ears aren't just for hearing. They are the primary way he cools down in hot weather.

Peter Rabbit can hop, but nothing like the hare. Hares, compared to rabbits, are the difference between your grade school runner and an Olympic champion. Hares' huge hind legs can propel them 10-20 feet in a single bound, and they can jump sideways and backward as well. Hares depend on speed to evade predators, and their speed is impressive—up to 40-50 miles per hour, all while twisting, jerking, and jumping in all directions. Your fastest coyote or fox can't compete with that.

Often in literature and mythology, the hare is portrayed as a trickster. Evasion is his superpower, and possibly due to his ability to jump, jinx, and turn on a dime, hares have been associated with trickster, magic, and witchcraft. John Lewis-Stemple writes:

> "As with many animals sacred to older religions, medieval Christians changed the hare into an animal of ill omen, saying witches shape-shifted into hare form to suck cows dry. Sailors considered hares so unlucky they could not be mentioned at sea. And not just sailors; country folk refused to call the hare by its name, opting for synonyms such as:
>
> Old turpin. . .the fast traveler, the way-beater. . .the nibbler. . .the cat of the wood . . .the hopper in the grass. . ."[1]

Also, his habit of eating his own feces is repellent to us. Unlike cows with several stomachs, hares (and rabbits) have trouble getting all their nutrients from their roughage diet of twigs, leaves, and bark, so they consume their soft poo for a full complement of vitamins. Then, they eliminate the hard pellets we usually associate with the rabbit in backyard hutches.

Hares prefer open country where they can forage, fornicate, and fight. And this is where the term "Mad as a March hare" comes from.

At dusk, dawn, and under the moonlight, hares can be seen racing around, jumping, jinxing, and boxing one another. They stand on their hind legs and rapidly, repeatedly box each other like miniature kangaroos. At first, this was thought to be about males determining dominance, like big horn sheep banging heads. But now we know this is actually a female letting the male know, "Not tonight, Harold! I'm not in the mood!" (whap-whap-whap).

After several sessions of flying over fields, jumping, pummeling, and boxing, the female picks the partner that has best stood up to her speed and abuse. Or maybe simply keeps coming back for more.

For centuries, this frenetic and goofy behavior has mystified people and given the hare a suspect reputation. Witchcraft, mythology, and much misunderstanding about hares have endured. What we have attributed as a magical and mysterious dance performed in secret under the moon by "mad" hares has been discovered as a normal mating ritual in the hare kingdom.

But author Lewis Carroll didn't know that when he penned *Alice in Wonderland* in 1865 and had the March hare join Alice and the Mad Hatter at the tea party. Alice remarks:

> *"The March Hare will be much the most interesting, and perhaps as this is May it won't be raving mad – at least not so mad as it was in March."*

I think Jesus would agree with Alice. Let's hang out with

the most interesting folks around; they're sure to entertain, and they're probably not as mad as we suppose.

The religious leaders thought the people Jesus liked to rub shoulders with were scandalous. The overlooked, the diseased, the idolaters, and the addicts didn't repel Him. He was accused of being a "glutton and a drunkard" (Luke 7:34) and certainly not sent from God if He was associating with these people. But He was mad for them, their passion, their desperation, their naked need that the religious leaders claimed was repellent. The only difference was that religious leaders could hide it better under layers of authority, power, wealth, and position.

And Jesus didn't just spend a few moments with them for image management or to grab the political sound bite. He ate, drank, and addressed their doubts, fears, and needs.

I always bristle when I hear people besmirching the Christian faith as a woman-hating patriarchal system. That might be true of their denomination or local church. But it's not true about Jesus. In a time when women had no rights, could not own property, and were all around dismissed, He healed them. He spent time and listened to them. He taught them alongside the men.

Who were the first people to hear about His resurrection from the dead? *Women.* Who did He appear to first after the resurrection? *Women.* Who did He notice and single out amid a crushing crowd for healing? *A woman.* For whom did He go out of his way to meet at a well? The Samaritan *woman.* Who did He first reveal His messianic identity to? That same woman. The love of God is mad for men, women, and anybody in between.

But we live in scary times. There is much to be suspicious and scared of. And many people who claim to be on the side of God seem waaaay off the mark in our eyes. Jesus' example is a simple ruler for how to be mad for the people He loved.

The healing of the leper in Luke 5: 12-16 reminds me of healthcare workers attending to the drug addicts on the streets. They clean and bandage infected and suppurating wounds of people who have no intention of "cleaning up their act."

The calling of Matthew the tax collector in Luke 5:27-32 happened while Matthew was still in his booth, serving the hated Roman government. No doubt the other disciples thought, "Are you sure about this? Do you know how much he oppresses our people by being on the side of the Romans? Isn't this a bit mad?" Yes, exactly.

The welcoming of the sinful woman in Luke 7 completely scandalized the rest of the dinner party when she came in and washed His feet with her perfume, tears, and hair.

Jesus demonstrated the mad, passionate, surprising love of God to all of us grubby, self-righteous, greedy, secret addicts, and addicted-to-power people.

Maybe God cares less about our orthodoxy than He does our loveability.

What we are not familiar with, we are uncomfortable with. And we tend to cling to our notions about the "right way" to approach God. We might want to confront our biases and entrenched views about who God loves and who and how He wants us to love.

A good start is just to fling our deluded selves into His arms, to be mad about Him, and to care less about crossing our t's and dotting our i's in our orthodoxy. The religious leaders were obsessed with laws, rules, and orthodoxy. Jesus was obsessed with wonder, worship, and welcoming people to His side. We can do the same.

In these powder keg political times, we are quick to label people as red or blue and "in" or "out" of the kingdom. We need to exchange this for seeing everyone on a path. Some are heading closer to God, and some are running the other way. They may turn around at some point, and they may go down rabbit trails of distraction (I've certainly done this). But we have no idea where they will end up. Only God knows. We are all finding our herky-jerky, jumpy, twisty-turning, battling way along the path.

In the meantime, maybe we could join everyone in the mystical and magical dance of life that God blesses all of us with.

Then, hopefully, on the last day of our lives, we can say, "I was mad as a March hare for God."

Moonlit Musings

1. Who are the most interesting and passionate or somewhat "mad" people you know?
2. What makes them interesting?
3. Were you brought up with a definite view of the "right way" to approach God? Do you still adhere to those practices or not?
4. How have you—or can you—demonstrate your passion for God?

Prayer

Heavenly Father,

I'm so grateful that your Son Jesus, who is "God with skin on" showed us how to love. Although sometimes I confess I want mercy for myself and justice for others, I am thankful you showed us what love really looks like. Open my eyes to where I am stingy with love. Show me where I pull back and fail to give you all of my heart. And help me to get to the point where I'm "mad as a March hare" for you.

In Jesus' name, amen.

---

[1] John Lewis-Stemple, The Running Hare (London: Transworld Publishers, 2016).

CHAPTER 16

Mosquito

I t's exasperating. You just manage to settle down for the night, and as your mind starts to unwind from the day, your muscles slowly begin to let go of all the stored tension, and you feel yourself drifting off. . . there it is.

Whine....whine...... Dang! There's a mosquito in the room, and you can't sleep until you find it. So, you flick on the light, and the hunt begins. Fortunately, they are slow fliers. They only fly at 1 to 1.5 miles per hour (which is snail-paced compared to the honeybee, which can reach 15 miles per hour). But still, you must find it, or there will be no sleep tonight. Besides, you can't bear the thought that this tiny thing you can flatten with your palm will be dipping into your life's blood as you rest.

As you stand motionless, wondering where it went, you also wonder, "Why does it keep bothering me? What's attracting it to me?" Those answers are various.

First of all, only the female mosquitoes want to bite you. The males never do. They are busy pollinating flowers. But a female needs protein for her eggs to develop, so she's out for blood. And that whining buzzing sound? That sound is her wings beating. They beat 300 to 600 times per second. No wonder you hear a whine.

Although they annoy most of us in North America, they are rarely truly scary. But for such a tiny insect, they can be surprisingly deadly. In fact, mosquitoes are the deadliest animal in the world. Worse than snakes, sharks, spiders, tigers, hippos, and anything else you can think of as scary, or at least with a reputation for death.

This is because mosquitoes, although tiny, can spread diseases like dengue fever, malaria, yellow fever, Zika, West Nile, chikungunya, malaria, and encephalitis. While these diseases are not 100% fatal, they still manage to kill 700,000 people every year and cause immense suffering. We used to associate this kind of disease with the deepest, darkest Africa. But that is no longer the case. Thanks to climate change, we are seeing some of these diseases in Hawaii, Texas, Florida, and other warm climes that are a little too close for comfort.

Dengue (pronounced "den-gay") usually produces somewhat mild symptoms of headache, rash, fever, and muscle and joint pain. But for others, it progresses to persistent vomiting, bleeding gums or nose, and enlarged liver, which needs to be treated as a medical emergency. The World Health Organization classifies the Dengue virus as one of the top ten global health threats. It is estimated that at least half of the world's population is at risk of infection.

Zika virus, while mild (fever, rash, headaches, muscle

pain), can be serious if pregnant. There is an increased risk of stillbirth, abortion, neurological disorders, or delivering children with birth defects. And there is no treatment available.

Yellow fever was the scourge that felled many sojourners and missionaries traveling to humid climates. It produces jaundice (yellow skin and eyes due to impaired liver function). When mild, it looks like the other diseases: fever, headaches, and chills, but then adds bleeding from the mouth, nose, eyes, or stomach. Approximately 50% of the small number of people who get severe symptoms will die within 10 days. While there is no cure, there *is* a vaccine. So, if you're traveling to warmer spots where it is prevalent, you might want to forego any reticence to vaccinations.

Chikungunya is the strangest virus to me. The name is derived from the Kimakonde language used in Tanzania and Mozambique, and it means "to become contorted." The symptoms start off like most: a rash, fatigue, headaches, and muscle and joint pain. Usually, these resolve in a week. But occasionally, an infection can morph into a severe fever and extremely painful joints, which lasts months or years, resulting in a hunched, contorted appearance.

At the head of the list is malaria. Female *Anopheles* mosquitoes transmit the disease, and estimates for the extent of cases worldwide are about 220 to 247 million. And the death rate from that is about 400,000. Each year. Symptoms include fever, headache, and chills (starting 10-15 days after the bite).

With all these awful diseases being spread by this tiny little insect, one has to wonder: what good are they? Can we not just wipe them off the face of the earth? That would be a mistake. Mosquitoes are pollinators. While bees get all the glory, mosquitoes pollinate as well. And they are integral to the food web. Bats, dragonflies, turtles, birds, and the most adored little bird—hummingbirds—rely on mosquitoes for their diet.

But sometimes, it feels like those other animals aren't eating enough of the dreaded insects. Or that we are the main prey for mosquitoes. Growing up in the Midwest, you get used to riding your bike with your mouth closed. You get used to having your windshield covered in bug guts. You get used to slamming the outside doors quickly. "Don't let the bugs in!" is the familiar cry.

Once, while on a canoe trip down the Wisconsin River, one of the women in our group had on a t-shirt that depicted a giant mosquito across her chest. Above it said, "Minnesota state bird." It got a lot of laughs, except for one guy. Possibly on the spectrum, he didn't get the joke and remonstrated her, "That's incorrect." The rest of us looked at him with gimlet eyes. When you know, you know.

While we were all setting up our tents along the banks of the river, a soft sunset began to bloom in innocent pink hues across the tranquil skies. And something else began to bloom in malevolent numbers. Huge, dense clouds of mosquitoes—10 feet across—swarmed after our blood. I'd never seen anything so huge as these massive clumps of whining, thirsty insects. It was surreal. Once we escaped into our tents, we could hear them like rain, pitter-pattering against the walls of our tent. It felt like the movies *Deliverance* and *The Birds* were mashups, and they became *The Mosquitoes*. That night, that guy became a believer.

How do mosquitoes seem to find us? It's like they have

a radar for where we are. Unless you can hold your breath, mosquitoes are going to find you. That's because they are attracted to your breath—the carbon dioxide we exhale. They can sense carbon dioxide from 50 yards away. This also explains why we often find them near our faces and ears as we drift off. We hear the whine because they are homing in on our exhalations.

I've been thinking a lot about my exhalations lately. While I've never subscribed to the metaphysical voodoo of "our words create our reality," there is power in the spoken word. God spoke the heavens and the earth into existence. We confess our faith—or lack of faith—with our words. Jesus defeated Satan's attempts to make Him give up His path by speaking words from scripture. The Bible is full of admonitions to watch our tongues; they are a restless evil that is quick to stir up trouble. Therefore, we do well to pay attention to them.

My husband is sometimes stunned by the thoughtless, faithless words that tumble out of my mouth. I think I'm just being honest about my struggles, but he sees it differently. He sees it as if I'm bringing forth more doubt, misery, and faithlessness upon my life by uttering them out loud. Almost as if I'm imbuing them with power. I'm not so sure about that, but I do see the truth of what Jesus said: "For the mouth speaks what the heart is full of" (Matthew 12:34).

That's why I was so convicted the day I saw—really saw—the black evil stored in my heart that was revealed by my thoughts.

I grew up in a family that championed competitiveness. Striving, getting A's, breaking records, or at least doing better than your peers was seen as primary importance. It was inculcated in me to rise to the top. So, in every situation, I constantly assess my standing in relation to others. And usually, I fared pretty well in comparison. But as we all know, there will always be someone richer, thinner, fitter, smarter, and more talented than you.

While I knew that jealousy, envy, and selfish ambition are warned against in the Bible (who am I kidding, it's compared to *idolatry*!), I didn't take my heart's condition seriously. I just thought I had a "competitive streak" and occasionally struggled with jealousy.

Therefore, I was shocked and stunned when I heard what came out of my heart one day leafing through a magazine. I was reading an article in a faith-based magazine and noted who the author was. "Hmmmm, she's been getting a lot of press lately, lots of social media mentions. It seems like everything she touches turns to gold. . .But you never know, her story isn't over yet. She might get derailed or get cancer."

The room became preternaturally silent, and everything around me seemed to fade from view. The usual chatter in my head, distant sounds, and the neighbor's barking dog faded. I was alone with those black thoughts hanging in the air like a poisonous, ominous, heavy presence.

It felt like the Holy Spirit leaned in close, looked me in the eyes, and quietly asked, "What did you just say?"

I blinked. With dawning horror, I realized that I had just wished death upon someone who was successful in an area I wanted to be. *What in the world?*

Years ago, a family relative, upon reading my first book, *Gardening Mercies*, closed it and told me, "Well, it's just a bit too personal for me." Meaning I had revealed too much. They were uncomfortable with my confessional explorations. I would so much like to be what Anne Lamott describes as "a somewhat Jesus-y bon vivant," but when I look back on the writings from others that have helped pull me from the pit of Hades, they are confessional. They are honest and show me I'm not alone. That others have these black thoughts, too.

My black heart isn't a surprise. "The heart is deceitful above all things, and desperately wicked; Who can know it?" said the prophet Jeremiah (chapter 17, verse 9 KJV). Who knows it? God does. We do not shock or surprise Him with our black thoughts of murder, jealousy, and all the other goblins from the pit. But we cannot claw ourselves upwards out of that slimy situation on our own. Or, even if we do, our hearts haven't changed; we just muscled our way through temporarily.

I saw so clearly the tiny little bite of competitiveness in my background that I had fed and nurtured throughout the years had spread a systemic disease of rampant jealousy, envy, and selfish ambition. What I thought was no big deal had twisted my heart and soul like one of those victims of the chikungunya virus. One who had "become contorted."

I dropped the magazine and flopped on the couch with my hands over my face. I felt like I had gazed over a mossy bank into a reflecting pool and found the face of one of the demonic goblins from *Lord of the Rings* staring back at me. I felt shaken and sick.

In tears, I confessed to my husband the sick condition of my soul. God bless him; he didn't bat an eye. "Yeah, I know," he said. "This has been a struggle for you for a long time." *He knew?* How could he not be repulsed by me?

It turns out I'm married to someone far above my station in life, and I'm forever grateful. He sees me through the eyes of Christ. He sees the winsome and wicked parts that need a lot of spiritual surgery.

Never before had I so identified with the apostle Paul's words,

> "So I find this law at work: Although I want to do good, evil is right there with me. For in my inner being I delight in God's law; but I see another law at work in me, waging war against the law of my mind and making me a prisoner of the law of sin at work within me. What a wretched man I am! Who will rescue me from this body that is subject to death? Thanks be to God, who delivers me through Jesus Christ our Lord!" (Romans 7:18-25).

In Chapter 8, Paul goes on to explain that we have a choice. We can live by flesh or by spirit. Flesh wants fame, fortune, and to rise above everyone else. Paradoxically, there's never enough of that drug to satisfy. Spirit wants life and peace and the sublime and beautiful things that flow from one who is connected to God through His Word and Spirit. So, we have a choice.

As much as I'd like to report that it's a one–and–done event, it's not. It's a walk. That's probably why the first-century followers of Jesus were called "People of The Way." It's a lifetime journey of choices to acknowledge our black hearts, offer them up to God in repentance, and choose His way going forward. Sometimes, it's several times a day.

We lurch forward, sideways, backward, and then stumble forward again. Along the way, we learn that it's not so much about getting stronger and better with experience and age as about becoming more dependent. After many miles along our own, personal pilgrimage, we see that we have been guided by grace. And grace will lead us home.

❦ · ❦

It's the small choices made poorly, weakly and daily through grace that truly change and transform even the debased.

❦ · ❦

I can't banish mosquitoes from my life forever nor hold my breath endlessly in their presence. And I can't make sure no seething and destructive thoughts ever enter my mind. But I can decide whether or not I will let them settle and sink in. I can "take every thought captive" (2 Corinthians 10:5). I can determine to take seriously their systemic effects when left unchecked and unconfessed.

I can choose to focus on all that God has blessed me with rather than what others have. Then, I can walk the path of faith with carefree confidence and trust that I'm being truly transformed from the inside, as opposed to a jaundiced, contorted faith that's just hobbling along. This allows me to truly celebrate how God is blessing other people's lives as well as mine.

It's a small choice, as small as a mosquito, and one that others will not see. But it will spread like a virus of good, infusing and releasing all parts of my contorted soul. And in relief and gratitude, I can exhale.

Moonlit Musings

1. What steps have you taken to avoid mosquitos where you live? Have you emptied out standing water under plants? Brought the dog bowl inside?
2. Have you ever been surprised by thoughts in your head? Thoughts of envy, jealousy, comparison? What do you usually do about those? Ignore? Confess?
3. Which of these verses helps you the most in tackling those thoughts? 2 Corinthians 10:4-5, Psalm 139:2, 1 John 1:9, Romans 7:18-25
4. Make a list of all the blessings you enjoy. Don't forget the basic ones we tend to take for granted—walking, seeing, hearing—as well as special ones such as friends, family, health, etc.

Prayer

Father God,

You see everything in my heart—even the slimiest, blackest thoughts. This is not who I want to be; this is not what you intended for me. I lift up to you my disordered desires, my "love of the world," my cravings for being noticed, my jealousies and envy, my stubbornness and pride. I give it all to you and ask you to cleanse me. Like Psalm 51:10 states, "Create in me a pure heart, O God, and renew a steadfast spirit within me." Thank you for your promise that "If we confess our sins, he is faithful and just and will forgive us our sins and purify us from all unrighteousness" (I John 1:9).

In Jesus' name, Amen.

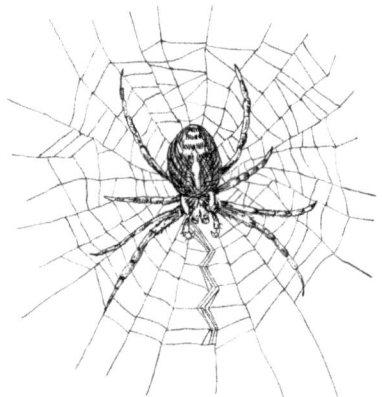

CHAPTER 17

Spider Web

S ummer evenings in our midwestern town were warm, languorous, and humid. After the sun had sunk in a coral and magenta splash behind the lake, the fireflies would come out. This was our invitation.

We neighborhood kids would run around, enjoying the evening breezes, dew-drenched grasses—slippery between our toes—and playing games in the last gasp of twilight. But occasionally, we'd hear a blood-curdling scream—sometimes combined with the sounds of choking and gagging.

The victim could be observed flailing about, wiping their face, spitting, spinning around, grunting, and repeating words such as "UGH!" and "Ewwww!" or "GROSSSS!!!" This is what I call the spider web dance. It expends about a week's worth of cardio in seconds.

It happens when an unsuspecting sojourner runs through the darkened landscape and suddenly finds his face has contacted a spider web stretched across his pathway. The sticky mass has adhered to his face, hair, and neck, and the victim imagines that somewhere on him is also a hungry spider. Hence, the dance.

Although we had heard stories of native Americans using spider webs to clot bleeding scrapes and wounds, this did nothing to allay our disgust at coming into such intimate contact with spider webs.

When I was older, I began to look at spider webs with an artist's eye, thanks to my grandmother. A serious photographer, she employed me to spray orb webs (those webs made by orb weaver spiders that look like spokes on a wheel with concentric rings). She wanted to recreate the look of early morning dew, so I dutifully sprayed them with water until each strand was laden with sparkling jewels of light-filled droplets. Then, she would capture their lacey, ethereal beauty with her Nikon. I developed a new appreciation for these spinners of art.

Not all spider webs are round. Some are large nets like you would see under trapeze performers. Others are funnels, some make triangles, and the Darwin's Bark spider from Madagascar can spray a continuous strand of silk 27 yards long. But my favorites are the orb weaver's round creations.

Chances are, if you're a fan of children's literature, you've already met a famous orb weaver spider—Charlotte, from E.B. White's *Charlotte's Web*. Apparently, Mr. White based his book on a spider he observed making her wonderous web in his barn.

I met my own orb weaver in the garden. Before dawn, while it was still pretty dark out, I got up early to do some gardening. I was leaning over some shrubbery, trying to cut back our window box geraniums that were done blooming. As I stretched over an expanse, something moved near my waistline. I looked down. In the middle of a perfect web that Charlotte could only dream of was a fantastic spider.

She was huge! About an inch long with a fat, plump body. And she was beautiful. Bright neon yellow bars covered the sides of her black body, with orange and black legs. I stepped back and considered. She straddled the center of her creation, which had an additional zigzag band of silk of about 3 inches that led directly to her. This zigzag part, the stabilmentum, was thought to help stabilize webs. Then scientists thought it was about making sure bigger things like birds didn't fly into and damage the webs. Scientists aren't united on why orb weavers make these zigzag portions in their webs. But some of them are amazing and intricate, and that's why these orb weavers are called "writing spiders."

My orb weaver was officially known as *Argiope aurantia*. There is another similar and maybe even more pretty one that is striped—or banded *Argiope trifasciata*. One Argiope spider that makes an amazingly intricate stabilmentum is the tropical *Argiope luzona*. Her web center is a mass of pronounced, intricate zigzags reminiscent of the artist M.C. Escher that seem to spin into infinity.

So, how do orb weaver spiders make these webs? To start with, all spiders can make silk, but not all spider silk is the same. Spiders can make up to seven kinds of silk, but most produce only four to five different types. The various kinds can consist of attachment silk, strong web frame silk (the outer structure), the orb web spiral line, sticky glue-like catching silk, swathing silk (for prey), and protective egg sac silk. They use this silk to make homes, catch food, protect their young, courtship, and even fly.

This silk is produced in silk glands, which travels as a liquid solution through long ducts to spinnerets, and at the end of these spinnerets are spigots. Contrary to what it looks like to our eyes, there is not *one* opening, making just one kind of silk. These spinnerets (they have several, usually in pairs of two or three) produce different kinds of silk. When silk is needed, by controlling the spigots (much like we do at our sinks), this fluid is compressed through the spigot's opening to create a solid silk thread.

And how does our Argiope spider construct her wheel-like creation? She begins with outer frame lines that are made of one kind of silk. Then she tackles the radial, spoke-like lines that will support the spiral sticky line (another type of silk) that makes up most of the web. The spiral line silk is much more elastic than the framework silk. Amazingly, the tensile strength is greater than that of mild steel and almost all artificial fibers. And when the web gets wet? The framing silk contracts to help keep the web tense and in shape.

The intricacy of these webs and their fragile but tenacious strength are impressive. But not as impressive as how often they build them. I always felt terrible tearing through a web while on a hike. I could imagine the spider thinking, "Well, thanks a lot. Took me days to construct that web, but you just plowed through it, and now I must start all over again." But now I know the truth: it takes them only about an hour to make one. Even more amazing is that after their web is torn or ruined, *they eat it*. In fact, some spiders eat their webs nearly every night before they build a new one. And it only takes about 30 minutes after being digested to have this raw material return to their silk glands to make more.

Their wasted webs are sustenance that fuels them to build again. Their ruin is their rejuvenation. Their busted plans are their food, their energy restorers. And so, they begin again.

For many of us, having our plans pummeled, dreams deferred, or hard work wasted is a disaster. We can barely survive it, much less think of starting again. We lie awake at night, ruminating over our failures, our dashed dreams. But under the starry skies each evening, our orb weaver merely lets the old web fuel her for the next one.

Some friends of ours with traditional jobs at big companies can't understand my husband. They have longevity, fat 401ks, and a long service reward in their future. Tom is a serial entrepreneur. Although he's taken two companies public, we have yet to make the zillions you so often hear about in Silicon Valley. And that's probably best because beginning again is what Tom does best. Is the last reiteration of the product not selling? He learns from that, pivots, and develops a new version. The previous company failed? He figures those are the odds of startups (1 in 10 are successful), and he begins again. Failure is never fatal, and the future is full of promise, fueled by his past experiences.

⊱⋅⊰

Our failures are never final,
they are fuel for moving forward.

⊱⋅⊰

When I am writhing in anguish over my besetting sins, behaviors, and lackluster performance, he reminds me to stop wallowing. "Looking back over those areas and getting lost in analysis paralysis isn't going to help you," he says. Pick up and move on." Start something new. Plan another product. Practice a different attitude. Because in moving forward, in practicing and beginning again, I develop a new outlook.

We don't expect a toddler learning to walk to give up after one attempt. They don't have the adult mindset of, "Well, I tried that, and it didn't work." They land on their diapered rumps, grin, and try again. And again, and again. The same approach is helpful to us. Begin again. We are, after all, just beginners at this thing called life. No matter how many years we've been at it, we learn and grow through a beginner's mindset.

I've had to learn this lesson over and over again, especially on my last book.

The publisher had said, "Your writing made us cry. It was so beautiful." Then they said they wanted to develop my career—we weren't going to do just one book together—they wanted to do a series! Probably three! Obviously, I was thrilled. But then the book came out with a typo on the back cover. Then, the Bible app they submitted my reading plan to had my name spelled wrong. Then they said, "Contrary to what we told you, we decided not to do another book with you." Disappointment, broken promises, dashed dreams, insecurity, and rage filled me. I stomped around the house with a massive bag of chips, mechanically stuffing them in my mouth as if a famine were due to start tomorrow. Then I had a lightbulb moment.

"Why am I standing here with a bag of chips in my hand, sabotaging myself? I'll show them!"

And I started painting. It was something utterly different than writing. It was a new, creative activity I couldn't compare to writing. I painted every day. I got better, much better. Although I had briefly flirted with being an art major in college, I hadn't pursued it beyond my freshman year. And now, decades later, I found solace and growth in this new-to-me watercolor experience. Then, I put my paintings on coffee cups, posters, and t-shirts and opened an online store. Then, I designed calendars, tea towels, and other creations that delighted my creative self. And people bought them. They posted glowing reviews, and my little bruised, creative self began to enjoy the journey again. Oddly enough, out of my discouragement, my best-selling product is a mug of bluebirds saying, "It's time for a cup of happiness."

But I probably wouldn't have discovered all that had I not gone through my disappointment. By letting my busted book dreams fuel me, I began again. And again, and again. Every day a new idea, a new painting, a new outlook.

Thomas Edison didn't ruminate on his failures to create the lightbulb. He said, "I have not failed 10,000 times—I've successfully found 10,000 ways that will not work."

God doesn't ruminate on our failures, either.

"As far as the east is from the west, so far has he removed our transgressions from us" says Psalm 103:12 .

And in Lamentations, we find,

> "Because of the Lord's great love we are not consumed, for his compassions never fail. They are new every morning; great is your faithfulness" (3:22-23).

My personal favorite is,

> "If we confess our sins, He is faithful and righteous to forgive us our sins and to cleanse us from all unrighteousness" (1 John: 1:9 NASB).

The apostle Paul showed us what this looks like in action;

> "Not that I have already obtained all this, or have already arrived at my goal, but I press on to take hold of that for which Christ Jesus took hold of me. Brothers and sisters, I do not consider myself yet to have taken hold of it. But one thing I do: Forgetting what is behind and straining toward what is ahead, I press on toward the goal to win the prize for which God has called me heavenward in Christ Jesus" (Philippians 3:12-14).

Or as Winston Churchill said, "Success is not final, failure is not fatal: it is the courage to continue that counts."

As you gaze up at your ceiling in the middle of the night rehearsing your hurts, think of our orb web weaver spider, calmly digesting her last web and making a new one. She doesn't bemoan the loss of her web—she lets it fuel her next one. Life is guaranteed to disappoint us. We will all have our broken web moments. Eat that web of disappointment and dashed dreams and begin again.

꙰·꙰

Let it fuel you forward ever, backward never.

꙰·꙰

Moonlit Musings

1. Have you had the unfortunate experience of running into spider webs?
2. What is your reaction towards spiders in general? Fear and loathing? Or fascination? Why do you think that is?
3. How do you react to projects and dreams falling apart? Does the spider's story of using failure for fuel inspire you? How could you mimic that?
4. Which of the verses listed above give you the most relief regarding the failures of your past?

Prayer

Father God,

Thank you for second chances, new mornings, and the promise of a new life in Christ. Help me overcome my disappointments and failures with renewed hope. Help me gain your perspective on events in the past. Help me see it all in the light of your eternal perspective. Thank you that my so-called limitations and roadblocks are nothing compared to your might and power. Give me courage and show me how to move forward and begin again with confidence in your benevolent care.

In Jesus' name, amen.

CHAPTER 18

Mockingbird

H*ow did I get here?* I chastised myself while watching the bedroom clock tick the hours away. One a.m., two a.m., three a.m., crawling by in the hush of nighttime. I was pinned to the pillow with looping thoughts of discouragement, anxiety, fears, frustrations, and the usual nighttime Nazgul ghost riders of doom thundering through my head.

In the yawning darkness of night, stillness envelopes our bedrooms and seems to amplify sounds, thoughts, and phantom futures as we watch the hours inch forward torturously slow. We rehearse what we said, what we should have said, what happened in the past, what might happen in the future, the odds of success, the futility of our futures... until getting up and partaking in hefty doses of carbohydrates sounds like the best solution.

I was convinced that WW3 was about to erupt, the nation was running out of food, our world was heading for a *Mad Max* apocalypse, the middle class was being decimated, and both political parties were run by sadistic saboteurs who thought nothing of the next generation. The American church was bowing to the god of nationalism and greed, and all definitions of good and evil were upside down and backwards. My talent was pathetic, my best years were behind me, my contribution to the kingdom of God laughable, and honestly, why try at all?

Trying to take myself in hand, I asked again, *How did I get here?* There had to be a trail, some mile markers I had followed to end up in such a state.

It had been a glorious day. My husband Tom and I enjoyed a hike with friends. Cobalt clear skies, low humidity, high visibility from the peaks to the ocean, and gorgeous fall foliage. I delighted in spying turkey tail mushrooms and quail feathers along the route. I heard the Steller's jays calls of, *Thief! Thief!* We were thrilled by the piercing scream of red-tailed hawks and the watery fluttering of quail in the bushes. We spotted a coyote loping up a distant hillside as we crested a hill. We chattered nonstop with our fascinating friends along the trails. So that was all good.

Or was it?

While the weather, nature, and vistas were all I could hope for, I thought about our conversations. Much of it had been about the sorry state of the economy, political climate, environment, nation, and general world. There were many, "Can you believe it's this bad?" and "What on earth are these people thinking? How can they be so gullible?"

And other diatribes on the sorry state of our nation. We *tsk-tsked* about the state of the church, its lack of sacrificial service, humility, and laying down of agendas. Our friends are smart. They are funny (in a snarky way). And they have big hearts. They *cared* about these things. Just as all of us who want to face a future of hope and promise care. But upon reflection, these conversations left me somewhat discouraged about the depressing state of the church, our nation, and the planet.

When we got home, our real estate agent left a message. Our bid on a house was far short of the winning offer—$400,000 over the asking price. The housing market showed us that it was laughable to think we could afford to buy a home in this area. This was no great surprise, but still, it was discouraging and frustrating.

Finally, I received an email of rejection for one of my writing projects. While I knew in my heart that it was often just a matter of what they had already published versus what their current needs were, I was hurt. My pride said they made a mistake. My insecurity said I was a trite and pathetic writer. I doubted God's care for me. I doubted that my creative talents had any hope for the future.

So. There had been some sign markers that led me to my pillow perusing. The conversations on the hike, the whirring in my brain over the myriad of concerns I had no control over, and random thoughts about my weight, health, and relationships. Like cells on a spreadsheet, I saw them neatly add up to the sum function: despair.

Then I heard the bird.

Interrupting my stream of bleak thoughts, spiraling through the darkness of the night, an incongruous melody of birdsong sinuously ribboned into our bedroom window. It stopped, changed, and began a new one. What kind of bird sings at night? Doesn't it know what time it is? I turned my head on the pillow and strained to hear more. An energetic warbling, almost comical in its enthusiasm, spun out from this little bird's heart.

Why would a bird sing in the middle of the night? Was this just another sign of depressing climate change?

Then I remembered. That tune spinner singing so cheerfully and enthusiastically with a vast repertoire of songs in the dark was a mockingbird.

The mockingbird is a fantastic mimic. Its Latin name is *Mimus polyglottos*. *Mimus* is Latin for "a mimic" and *polyglottos* is Greek for "many-tongued." Native Americans in South Carolina called this bird the one with four hundred tongues. They've been known to mimic other bird songs as well as rusty gate hinges, baby cries, dog barks, and cellular phone rings. A mockingbird can imitate as many as thirty-two other species within ten minutes. This is because of the company he keeps.

After mockingbirds migrate from South America to North America each spring, ornithologists (scientists who study birds) have witnessed scraps of bird songs indigenous to that area coming out of the mockingbird's repertoire. So, if our grey-suited bird with a long tail and white patches on his wings hangs out with warblers, he will warble. If he hangs out with thrushes (like robins), he will sing with flute-like, liquid notes. He will sing the songs of those he spends the most time with.

But why was this mockingbird singing in the middle of the night? Was his circadian rhythm completely messed up? Was he confused about his time zone? No, he was singing out of desperation.

He's basically a lonely bachelor desperate for companionship. If a male mockingbird doesn't find a female in the spring, he will continue to try to attract one before the breeding season is over by singing all night long. In the stillness of the night, out pours his heart in warbling songs of love, calls of companionship, and promises of protection, if only someone will listen.

Stoically and resolutely, he will sing through the dark. He refuses to give up despite not seeing any hope on the horizon. He continues to pour forth beguiling notes of possible love and promises of a sweet future.

That night, when I was beset by worries and fears, hearing the mockingbird lifted my heart. His lonesome trills and songs have a tender poignancy. He tells me that I am not alone. His songs of longing reflect my own longing to know that God hears me when I cry out in the night.

In the dark times of our lives, it is greatly comforting to have someone in our lives who will sing to us encouraging words. Someone who will remind us that our current situation is not a permanent sentence over the rest of our lives. Someone who resolutely sings stories of hope, possibilities, and promising futures despite our naysaying.

I'm eternally thankful that my husband refuses to join me in my cesspools of despair. He steadfastly always chooses hope. And so does my friend Laura. She might sit in stunned silence as I rail on the phone about how dark everything is, but then she reminds me of past victories. She reminds me of God's promises. They both give me firm handholds to help me heft myself out of the slough of despondency.

But their ability to lift my spirits will depend on who influences them. Who are they listening to? What are they reading? These choices inform their outlook, and so influence mine.

Listening to words on the hike that constantly focused on the sorry state of the world sucked out any guileless hope I had. The beautiful afternoon had been glazed with a sense of, "Don't get too happy. Look at the reality." Hanging out with anyone who speaks a constant refrain of doom and gloom affects our outlook on life. And by listening to them, it was affecting mine.

I have a black belt in conjuring up all sorts of miseries and tragedies on my own in the middle of an interminable night. I don't need someone else to add to my sense of hopelessness. I can do that with a few flicks of my finger, doom-scrolling YouTube and the news.

Just like the mockingbird is influenced by the company he keeps, so am I. Do my influencers constantly complain about things? Or do they speak words of optimism and inspiration? I'm not expecting a syrupy-chirping, "Everything's awesome!" nauseating refrain, but my soul requires some encouragement and hope.

Hope is God's native tongue. His repertoire is vast, and He speaks through many different people and circumstances on how to find encouragement and hope. Thankfully, He didn't just hand down some decrees and then announce that we are on our own and good luck with all that. He tells us repeatedly in the Bible how important it is to lift each other up.

In 1 Thessalonians, the apostle Paul writes:

"For God did not appoint us to suffer wrath but to receive salvation through our Lord Jesus Christ. He died for us so that, whether we are awake or asleep, we may live together with him. *Therefore encourage one another and build each other up*, just as in fact you are doing" (chapter 5, verses 9-11, NIV, emphasis the author's).

Mutual edification—encouragement—is stressed in the book of Romans:

"Let us therefore make *every effort to do what leads to peace and to mutual edification*" (Romans 14:19, emphasis the author's).

For me, that means:

1. Break the habit of doom-scrolling online
2. Don't pass along snarky or mean-spirited memes
3. Refuse to be a part of long conversations about how "they" are ruining our nation
4. Stop allowing faithless words of hopelessness to pass my lips, no matter what circumstances I find myself in

I have to confess, some of these are real killjoys. Who doesn't love a perfectly executed, snarky meme? Who doesn't delight in someone's comeuppance? Well, my hand is up; I'll admit it. But when I read His Word, I have a choice. This displeases Him, hinders my spiritual growth, and contributes to a sour outlook. This leads to tossing and turning on the pillow with thoughts of, *"How did I get here?"*

The way out for me is mainly to watch my tongue. Unlike the mockingbird, I can easily slip into a singular refrain: *We are up a creek without a paddle.*

"The soothing tongue is a tree of life,
    but a perverse tongue crushes the spirit"
(Proverbs 15:4).

James, the brother of Jesus, wrote the definitive words about the power of the tongue. He writes:

> "Those who consider themselves religious and yet do not keep a tight rein on their tongues deceive themselves, and their religion is worthless" (James 1:26).

> "With the tongue we praise our Lord and Father, and with it we curse human beings, who have been made in God's likeness. Out of the same mouth come praise and cursing. My brothers and sisters, this should not be. Can both fresh water and salt water flow from the same spring?" (James 3:9-11).

I think in the USA, we like to have an intellectual knowledge of God but keep our thoughts, attitudes, and behaviors in our pockets—like Bilbo's precious ring—to do with what we want. God wants us to empty our pockets and put it all on the table. And he, like Gandalf, will mercifully take it away because it is unhealthy for us. It is our downfall. It renders our outlook twisted and our tongue anything but tamed.

The fruit of our influencers and ourselves is in the tongue. It tells the world what's in the well of our souls.

When we use our tongues to edify and bless,
it helps pull us out of our misery and mess.

"A good man brings good things out of the good stored up in his heart, and an evil man brings evil things out of the evil stored up in his heart. For the mouth speaks what the heart is full of" (Luke 6:45).

In the book *To Kill a Mockingbird*, the young girl named Scout is told that "It's a sin to kill a mockingbird" because "Mockingbirds don't do one thing but make music for us to enjoy. . . but sing their hearts out for us. That's why it's a sin to kill a mockingbird."

In the dark times of our lives, we need to strain our ears for the mockingbirds. It might be a spouse, a friend on the phone, or time alone in the Psalms. We all need someone to sing incongruous hope into our souls, no matter how long and opaque the night. And we can do this for others. It might be a sin not to.

Moonlit Musings

1. What events, thoughts, or triggers get you tossing on your pillow at night?
2. Who in your life speaks hopeful, encouraging words more than doom and gloom?
3. Who do you know that tends to have an Eeyore

outlook—always expecting the worst? How does it feel to listen to them?

4. Who could you encourage with songs of encouragement?

Prayer

Heavely Father,

Your Word is full of encouragement and blessings. Help me to be a blessing to others with my words. It's so easy to fall in step with the snarky and critical, but that doesn't bless anyone. You said the "fruit of the Spirit is love, joy, peace, forbearance, kindness, goodness, faithfulness, gentleness and self-control" (Galatians 5:22). Well I need self-control. And probably some joy and kindness too. Show me how to sing hopeful songs to friends and family in dark times.

In Jesus' name, amen

CHAPTER 19

Migration

In the quiet of our darkened bedrooms with our heads on pillows, we try to ignore—or at least quell—the pinball of ricocheting thoughts about the day. Conversations, actions, inaction, plans, desires, frustrations, or savored small victories in our hearts all clamor to be heard as we try to settle down. Although we may be physically and emotionally exhausted, oftentimes that message hasn't made it to our blue-light saturated eyes and brain cells. The detritus of the day squawks, whispers, and clangs around our cerebellum and behind our eyelids as we pursue peaceful sleep.

Outside, we assume all the animals are settling down. Most are. The family dog has picked his spot, and he is securely snoozing. The cows and sheep are stilled in the pastures and pens. The sea otters hold hands while dozing and floating on the Pacific swells. And the Milky Way is frosting its way over the sparkling arc of the heavens.

But all is not still. Outside over our heads, on certain nights, there is a mass movement undetected by most of us about to begin.

Our beloved visitors to bird feeders are rustling their feathers in anticipation. They've waited until the evening because it's safer. Then furtively, in singles, then hundreds, and even thousands of sparrows, warblers, orioles, thrushes and ducks—just to name a few—are taking flight under cover of darkness.

This is the unseen yet enormous night migration of birds. While we may have seen and heard honking geese flying south in V's as we rake leaves in the fall, the nighttime migration is mostly a mystery to us. Why have they waited until night? Which birds do this? How many do this? And why do so many hit buildings at night? These mysteries are slowly unfolding to scientists as they employ radar and sensitive audio equipment to track their movements.

The migration happens at night for several reasons. There is less chance predators will threaten them. (Flocks of songbirds during the day would be a hawk's buffet.) The air has cooled by the evening, so they won't get exhausted as quickly. The wind currents have also dropped, ensuring less strain and an easier passage.

But flying at night is becoming more dangerous. Lights on buildings and towers confuse and disorient birds, causing them to crash in the hundreds on a single night. Every year, radio, TV, and cell towers account for seven million collisions in North America. Thankfully, some cities (New

York, Chicago, and Houston) are employing a "lights out" program during key bird migration times in the Fall and Spring. Hopefully, as scientists learn more about how birds navigate through city landscapes, the data could result in designing urban topography in ways that reduce danger.

Pinpointing just who is traveling where by night has eluded scientists for millennia. But they are getting closer to the answers. While it is primarily an unseen event, it is not a silent one, and that is becoming the key to discovery.

Most birds vocalize while on the wing, but these calls and sounds are nothing like the melodic music we are used to hearing in our backyards and forest walks. The sounds they make as they flow across our continent after dark are barely discernible and cryptic calls, chirps, tweets, whistles, and buzzes. Each of these vocalizations is particular to certain birds. Specialized acoustic monitoring equipment that can record, analyze, and identify these calls are being used by scientists to study their calls and movements.

This acoustic equipment—particularly microphones calibrated for recording nighttime migrants—can capture the high-frequency note of a particular bird flying 1,000 feet overhead. And they are becoming so affordable that enthusiastic birders add them to their wish lists next to binoculars.

While birds are a well-documented nighttime migration, they are not the only ones. By accident, on a June night in 2019, meteorologists at the National Weather Service saw something strange on their radar. It looked like a broad band of rain—nearly ten miles wide—but there were no clouds. An amateur weather spotter was contacted who was right under the mysterious object. He reported he wasn't getting rained on. He was seeing ladybugs. Millions of ladybugs.

Their radar had located a dense blanket of ladybugs floating 5,000 to 9,000 feet in the air. Despite its enormity, the swarm of ladybugs dissipated and disappeared into the night, and they lost track of it.

It's easy to see millions of caribou or wildebeests moving en masse as they migrate during the day, but not so much our nighttime migrators. Yet these midnight movements are no less impressive and significant.

There is another significant, massive migration taking place under cover of darkness. Quietly and mysteriously, hearts are fluttering with hope in the Middle East.

People are whispering to each other about dreams they've had. Very detailed dreams about Jesus. He is appearing to people who have no knowledge of Him and causing a tsunami of revival.

It doesn't matter if you make a specific religion illegal. It doesn't matter if you make leaving Islam a death sentence. It doesn't matter if you live in a country without churches, radio, internet, or TV about Jesus. He will find open hearts and reach them. So faith in Jesus Christ is quietly migrating and exploding in the hearts and minds of people in Iran, Iraq, even the center of Muslim pilgrimage—Mecca, Saudi Arabia—and under other oppressive regimes.

Under the blanket of darkness, they meet in underground churches. Everyone surrenders their phones, the batteries are removed, and tossed into a pile under a heap of clothes. They whisper and talk about Jesus. There is an unquenchable fire in their hearts, and they understand that they might die for this.

While watching the documentary *Sheep Among Wolves*, I was astonished at what the men asked their wives. One said, "If they come for us and are raping you, what will you do? What do you want me to do? His wife replied, "Pray and do nothing. It's the least I can offer Jesus. I said He can have my life, that includes my body too." They rehearse in their minds their loved ones being tortured. They rehearse all the very real possibilities of what it might mean to follow Jesus in their country. They are migrating into the realm of what the first-century Christians endured, where nothing is guaranteed, secure, or predictable except for persecution. And they wouldn't change it.

On Jennie Allen's podcast, *Made For This*, she interviewed a man from the underground church, and he talked about how his wife wanted to leave the United States and return to the Middle East. He said, "Why on earth go back to that?" She said, "Because the church here is under a satanic lullaby, and I'm falling asleep. And every time I try to wake up, the lullaby goes faster."

She didn't want the lullaby of our comfy, cushy Western lives to rob her of the immediacy, urgency, and vitality of knowing Jesus and seeing His power and love migrate across her land.

Here in the West, it's unthinkable to migrate from one side of the political aisle to the other. It takes counsel with friends to just migrate back home for Thanksgiving. And it can be scary to migrate in our beliefs inside the secret chambers of our hearts.

Under cover of darkness, alone in our thoughts, we reevaluate our opinions, beliefs, and values. Our close friends, spouses, and families don't know what's transpiring in the hidden recesses of our hearts and minds, but we do. And those thoughts disquiet us.

How will people respond? Will they be inquisitive and want to know why we are considering migrating? Even if we know others berating our thoughts and considerations is usually based on fears and upsetting the balance, it's still challenging to face being labeled "wrong" and "crazy" for considering a different point of view.

My husband and I come from different sides of the aisle politically. When discussing politics, he brings in the Biblical point of view—like taking care of the poor and loving your enemies. My opinions therefore sometimes migrate and seesaw. But while I'm trying to pick a side—or which party has the better answer for an issue—he always shakes his head and says, "Face it. We are in Babylon. It doesn't really matter. No political party is going to save this nation. Just do what Jesus said." And I migrate back to where I should be.

But it can make me uncomfortable. I'm far happier when I can give mental assent to theology, doxology, and Biblical facts but not make it change my lifestyle, priorities, prayers, giving, or spending.

He thinks the evangelical church gets too wrapped around the axle about people's personal lives and whose theology is right or wrong. He points out that the Bible talks about taking care of the poor and disadvantaged far more than our current topics of angst. My husband is very much a "red letter" Bible reader (some Bibles have Jesus' words printed in red text). Meaning, he actually reads and pays attention to what Jesus said and doesn't see it as philosophy, Christology, orthodoxy, or theology but more "do-ology." As in, *do it.* This can be disruptive to your politics, priorities, and personal habits.

❀

*Maybe following Jesus is less about orthodoxy
and theology and more about do-ology.
As in, "Just do it."*

❀

Personally, I don't like giving until it hurts (I was eyeing a new e-bike, darn it). I prioritized selling some extra things in the garage and buying others (he suggested we give them away to bless local farm workers). Politically, I am suspect as to whether all homeless people are hapless victims or habitual poor choosers (he says it doesn't matter, give anyway). And the longer I've been married to him—32 years so far—the more convicted I am about Jesus' words.

They are starkly inescapable and uncomfortable.

While I might talk about an alarm system for a future house, he reminds me of *Les Misérables* where the priest gives the thief more silver candlesticks. "Offer them your shirt too," Tom says (see Luke 6:29).

While I might eye illegal migrants as opportunists, he'll say, "Welcome the stranger" (see Matthew 25:34-36).

And while I am desperate to become homeowners again he reminds me, "Jesus didn't have a place to lay his head. Don't worry about it" (see Luke 9).

I admit that sometimes it feels like I'm married to the Dalai Lama, Mary Poppins, and Billy Graham all in one. I want to slap him. I want to yell, "What about what I want?!! Is it so wrong for a woman to want a home?!!"

Although I'm 3 inches taller than him and can be quite

vociferous, he is undeterred. He tilts his head, smiles, and spreads out his hands. "Just what is so awful about your life right now? You have perfect health. You have no debts. Your husband adores you, cooks for you, and you have a roof over your head. What's to complain about?" What can I say in the wake of current wars, pestilence, and political upheaval? Nothing.

In the West, we think our unmet needs and greed are akin to "carrying our cross" and "dying to ourselves." It's not. It's not even close.

After watching *Sheep Among Wolves*, I realized that their very real possibility of martyrdom is a slap in our slack-faith faces. Because they don't have "bullets, beer, and bread," they are able to see Jesus actually supply their very real needs supernaturally—something we in the West don't need or see much. How can we migrate in our hearts to where they are? To complete dependency on Jesus?

Sometimes the greatest migration we can go through is to have something we know intellectually in our heads drop down 18 inches into our heart of belief.

When Jesus came on the scene, the people were looking for a Savior to overthrow the oppressive Roman government. They mistakenly thought He had come to get involved in politics and set things right for the people. He didn't and wouldn't use political means to accomplish His kingdom. Yet we are still looking in vain for that earthly Savior to make things right for our side of the aisle.

1. Jesus said we had to lay down our rights and put others first. (Matthew 5:38-40)
2. Jesus told us to take up our cross—an instrument of torture and death. (Mark 8:34)

3. Jesus wants us to be fishers of men's souls, not caught up in politics. (Matthew 12:13-17)
4. Jesus admonishes us that the right side of any issue is with Him. (Matthew 12:30)

The religious leader Nicodemus slunk around to meet with Jesus under cover of darkness. He didn't want anyone—particularly those in power—to witness the migration happening in his heart. But he had some inkling that Jesus had the answers.

I think when the truths of Jesus's red-letter words migrate from our heads to our hearts, there will be a massive migration of souls on this earth. There will be less division. Like migrating birds, we might call out little chirps of encouragement to each other along our journeys, no matter where we are headed. When those who are called by His name humble themselves and pray en masse, He will heal our land. And we will migrate closer to Jesus' side of the aisle, the kingdom of God.

Moonlit Musings

1. Have you ever witnessed birds migrating at night? (Did you know reptiles do this too on early spring, rainy nights?)
2. Are there any social issues you had to migrate to a different viewpoint about after getting more information in your political views? Are you open to that?
3. Why do you think a well-known and respected leader like Nicodemus came to Jesus under cover of darkness? What was he afraid of?
4. Does it make you nervous to consider applying some of the words and admonishments of Jesus?

Prayer

Heavenly Father,

The faith of our Middle Eastern brothers and sisters under persecution humbles me. I have never had to risk my life for my faith. But many around the world do. Remind me to pray for the persecuted church. And most of all, show me how to live out Jesus' words in my home and community. You certainly didn't send him to die for me to give me the cushiest life possible. Help me to migrate away from selfishness and ingest his words and actions into my heart so I can love and sacrifice like he did.

In Jesus' name, amen.

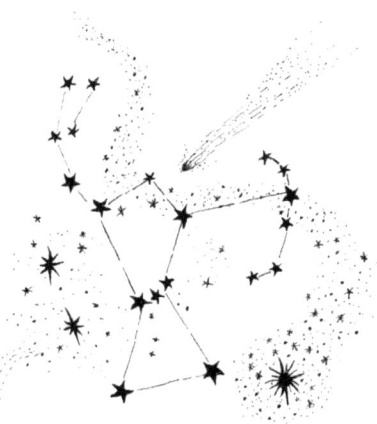

Stars

J ohn fiddled with and adjusted the knobs and dials on his telescope. He squinted through the lenses while I glanced up and down the dark streets like a rabbit exposed in the middle of the road. Because, in fact, we were in the middle of the road. It was a warm summer evening in Palo Alto, California, and my friend, who was in the astronaut program at NASA, determined that this was the best place to show me the stars.

"Here," he said, "look through here. You can see the constellation of Pleiades. You know, of course, that this constellation is mentioned in the Bible—in the book of Job, where God speaks of His authority and asks, 'Can you bind the chains of the Pleiades?'" (Job 38:31).

I didn't know that, but since we were part of the same Bible study, I felt I should have. I peered through the lenses at the twinkling pinpricks of light, then straightened up and looked at John. "So you're telling me I'm looking at the exact same stars as they were two thousand years ago?" I asked.

John smiled at me indulgently. "Well, technically, longer than two thousand years ago—Job was written before Jesus's time. And the universe is expanding...but yes, the same."

John went on to describe different types of stars— dwarfs, giants, supergiants—and their different luminosities. Their colors can be red, orange, yellow, blue, or white. They have names from antiquity, like Sirius, and crazy-sounding names, like Betelgeuse. Then he described how stars are formed. They start out in a state of clouds and dust and gases. Then a star's own gravity causes it to collapse in on itself, so the center becomes denser and hotter from pressure. Particles start to stick together and then fuse—which becomes the energy source of the star. It "switches on" and begins to shine. The hydrogen atoms fuse and become helium. This nuclear fusion creates the energy that powers every star. He went on to describe how some stars are more massive than our sun, and that they fuse heavier and heavier elements—all the way up to iron—and then have an iron core. At which point they have no more energy from fusion, and over time they collapse in on themselves and end up in a massive supernova explosion.

My brain was collapsing in on itself and about to explode with this tsunami of astrophysics, but I got back on track when he said, "Scientists believe that all the elements in our periodic table were all created inside a star, from the fusion of helium and hydrogen, and then dispersed in the explosion—the Big Bang." Now that was compelling. One massive, energetic, creative moment from which all the building blocks of matter were created. It's fascinating how science and faith can intertwine in lyrical dance.

But all this star talk was a bit too academic for my tastes. While it was impressive and dazzling, I prefer the romance of stars and how they hint at a loving and imaginative Creator. I like to think of His hand scattering the confetti of brilliance across the carpet of sky. I like to ponder God's immensity, artistry, and care for the great and small things He has made. The psalmist said, "When I consider your heavens, the work of your fingers, the moon and the stars, which you have set in place, what is mankind that you are mindful of them, human beings that you care for them? You have made them a little lower than the angels and crowned them with glory and honor" (Psalm 8:3-5). And again, the psalmist remarks, "He determines the number of the stars and calls them each by name" (Psalm 147:4).

They may have been formed by gases and nuclear fusion all in a big bang, but that doesn't mean He didn't set the forces in motion, nor does it make them any less enchanting and poetic.

I like to ponder God's immensity, artistry, and care for the great and small things He has made.

It's been said that Tycho Brahe, the brilliant Danish astronomer who built on Copernicus's heliocentric universe and paved the way for astronomers Kepler and Galileo in the 1600s, said, "Those who study the stars have God for a teacher."

Which is basically what Psalm 19:1 says: "The heavens

declare the glory of God; the skies proclaim the work of his hands."

Although star creation consists of powerful cycles of elements fusing and growing, exploding in a tug-of-war between gravity and energy, the science begets contemplative wonder and delight. I love the quote by Ralph Waldo Emerson: "If the stars should appear one night in a thousand years, how would men believe and adore, and preserve for many generations the remembrance of the city of God which had been shown!"

From recorded history, the stars have been the object of curiosity, omens, romance, verse, mystery, and delight. Cave paintings in Europe that date back 10,000 years depict their formations. Their varied arrangements—which we sort into constellations such as Orion (the hunter) or the Bear (which includes the Big Dipper)—are usually easily seen, even if you live near a bright, modern city.

In the San Francisco Bay Area, with a population of seven million people and an ever-present ambient light spray, John and I needed a telescope to look past the city glow to find our Pleiades constellation. The best night-sky viewing is done in the absence of light pollution, which is why serious observatories around the world are in remote locations. The darker your surroundings, the more dazzling will be the stars in the sky.

But it's getting harder to find dark places in which we can be dazzled. Although most of us are aware of the plastics filling up our oceans (as well as pollution of other sorts), few realize the light pollution that is filling our nighttime skies. The Dark Sky Initiative and other similar organizations are working to change this. They point out that most of our cities' light litter is from streetlights. That glow you see in the sky surrounding urban areas? That's because the light particles from streetlights are scattered by the atmosphere, which creates the glow across the landscape. This could be greatly mitigated by shielded, downward-facing lights.

But is this really a problem? So what if there's a glow around our lit-up areas? Here's something to think about. Light pollution causes migrating birds to crash into buildings. Just-hatched sea turtles mistake the glow of streetlights for the moon shimmering on the ocean and head inland, where they are crushed by cars. And then there's the waste. Lighting up the nighttime wastes money and fossil fuels. To keep a 100-watt lightbulb turned on for a year takes the equivalent energy output of a half ton of coal. With the switch to more efficient LED lights, cities have gotten even brighter, obliterating the chance to view the night-sky wonders. In fact, scientists from the Light Pollution Science and Technology Institute in Italy say the Milky Way is no longer visible to more than a third of the world's population.

In my teenage years, it drove me crazy that my father was always turning off lights in the house and commenting on how much money we were wasting. I would think, "What's the big deal over a few lightbulbs?" Combined with those of everyone else in the world, it is a big deal. I want my son to be able to see the Milky Way. I want others around the world to experience the glorious display of the evening star show by simply stepping outside, without the need of telescopes.

———————

Years after my experience with John, I didn't need a telescope to be mesmerized by the starry night. I was working in Australia with an ad agency, and we were scouting out locations for a photo shoot in the middle of nowhere—the outback of the Northern Territory, to be exact.

I didn't want to breathe too deeply; it hurt too much. The kiln-like air muffled all desire for movement. There was no cooling sweat to be had as the punishing, arid sun slammed down on the surrounding boulders and our necks. We tried to huddle in the scant shade of a large rock, but even there the temperature was 104 degrees. Usually, I'm quite cranky when I'm overheated, but I was incapable of being irritable in this heat; it just sucked the life force out of me. I looked out across the desiccated landscape and wondered for the hundredth time, *How do people live in this place? Why would they want to live here?*

This place was appropriately named Devils Marbles, and it was about 50 miles from a spit of a town called Tennant Creek, nearly in the center of the Australian outback. The "marbles" are massive, red-granite boulders—some up to 20 feet across—incongruously stacked and balanced in the middle of a flat, arid desert. We were there to shoot a magazine layout for Telecom Australia (now Telstra), depicting that even way out there, back of beyond, there was phone service.

After scouting out the location, we all headed back to the local motel. Our photographer told us we had to be back out there the next day by 4:00 a.m. because he wanted to capture the early-morning dawn against the massive red boulders. So, that next "morning" we staggered to the cars at 3:30. I slumped down in the backseat, trying to catch a few more winks. A short drive later, in the black stillness of the outback, devoid of civilization's lights, we arrived at

Devils Marbles. My workmate Dean got out of the car and said, "Wow… wow!" And then, "Get up, Laurie, you have to see this."

"Go away." I didn't like mornings any more than heat, and actually, it was too early to be morning yet. So, no, on both counts.

Dean's shoes softly crunched the dusty gravel as he slowly walked around the car in the dark. "Seriously," he said, "Get up!" He kicked at my shoe dangling over the edge of the seat.

"Awright!" I snapped and pushed myself up off the backseat. I heaved my hardly awake self upright next to the car and glared at Dean. "What?" He looked skyward, and I followed his gaze.

Miles from anywhere and with no ambient light, a deep black, Arabian night sky twinkled with an impossible carpet of diamonds winking back at me. The Milky Way was clearly defined, boldly rending the heavens with its distinguishable swath of billions and billions of tightly clustered lights. The Southern Cross, viewable only in the Southern Hemisphere, blazed in the sky like it does on the crisp blue Australian flag.

I blinked in astonishment. "Ohhhhh," I said. I had never seen stars that clearly. In the absence of lights and civilization's glow, it felt like you could reach out and touch them. They seemed to be benevolently hovering, tantalizingly close and full of mysterious, twinkling wonderment. I understood now why the ancients had spent so much time arranging the stars into constellations and making up stories about them. In the absence of electricity's glow, this enfolding darkness unveiled secrets worthy of such scrutiny and stories.

※･※

*I understood now why the ancients had spent
so much time arranging the stars into
constellations and making up stories about them.*

※･※

Here's another secret about the stars: The light we see
from the stars is not instantaneous. Meaning it has traveled
many light-years to get to us. So, as we look at the constellations, we are actually looking back in history. We are seeing
light that left those stars light-years ago. (A light-year is
5.88 trillion miles.) When you know how many light-years
away a star is, you subtract that number from the current
year. When we gaze up at Orion's belt, the star on the far
right, Mintaka, is 916 light-years away. So, the light we are
seeing left that star around AD 1109 (Current year: 2025
- 916= 1109). Sigurd I of Norway becomes the first Norwegian king to embark on a crusade to the Holy Land.

If you're reading this in 2026, the light you see from that
star is from 1110, King Henry I is making improvements
on Windsor Castle.

The light from the star on the far left of the three on
Orion's belt, Alnitak, is 817 light-years away. Therefore, (if
you're reading this in 2025) the light we see is from about
the year AD 1208. Otto IV is elected as king of Germany,
and travels to Milan to receive the Iron Crown and the
title King of Italy. And the Big Dipper? The last star in the
handle is named Alkaid. Since it is 104 light years away, its
light left around 1921—Woodrow Wilson is president and
Prohibition has been underway since 1920.

Above all else, I love the egalitarianism of stars. The fact that kings, mothers, children, and the homeless are privy to the same view satisfies me. In this world of increasing disparity between rich and poor, as the chasm yawns ever wider, I like it that we all can enjoy front-row seats to God's magnificent light show. Stars are for everybody. Rich or poor, First World or two-thirds world, black or white, we all have the same opportunity to view them. They don't shine any brighter for a world leader or a gang member. The stars remind me of God's love. It's always there, whether or not you can see or feel it, and it doesn't beam down differently for the church leader or the drug user. "The ground is level at the foot of the cross," the old saying goes, which is an egalitarian view of God's grace. There is no high or low standing when we are all standing there.

꒰ꞏ꒱

The stars remind me of God's love. It's always there, whether or not you can see or feel it, and it doesn't beam down differently for the church leader or the drug user.

꒰ꞏ꒱

In Jenna Bush Hager's winsome and heartwarming book, *Everything Beautiful in Its Time*, she talks about the importance of living joyfully and serendipitously. In her list of things like, "Smile at every baby you see," and, if anyone spills something, yell "Happy Days!" to remind everyone not to sweat the small stuff, there was my favorite: "Get out of bed to go look at the stars." She reminds me to take time to ponder the majesty that surrounds us—even when it's inconvenient.

The more I know about God's starry masterpiece, the more I want to find dark skies to sit under and ponder it. Now I understand the truth and meaning of John Muir's insight: "When we contemplate the whole globe as one great dewdrop, striped and dotted with continents and islands, flying through space with other stars all singing and shining together as one, the whole universe appears as an infinite storm of beauty."

That night in the Australian outback, while our photographer scrambled around scouting for the best angle before the coming of sunrise, I kept my head back and marveled at the celestial jewels overhead and their infinite storm of beauty. How extraordinary that in a dry and desiccated place named for the devil, I could behold the artistry of the heavens.

Moonlit Musings

1. When have you had a moment on vacation or away from cities where you saw the stars clearly? What impression did that make?

2. Read Psalm 8. What verses resonate with you the most?

3. What in God's creation fills you with the most awe? Have you ever been in a "dry and desiccated place" and yet still beheld beauty?

4. How does the thought that "the ground is level at the foot of the cross" make you feel about your own situation or about other people?

Prayer

Heavenly Father,

Thank you for Your artistry, for the amazing splendor of the Milky Way. I can only imagine how it dazzled ancient people with no ambient light to compete with it. Please remind me to stop for serendipitous moments to appreciate your creation—bare feet in the grass, the smell of the rose, and, of course, the brilliance of the night sky. Thank you that most of your beautiful design and creativity are on display (and free!) for us to see, enjoy, and ponder. Help me stop and notice what I usually take for granted.

In Jesus' name, amen.

CHAPTER 21

Sounds of Silence

Silence can be noisy. Ask any child alone in their bedroom at night. Once the clatter and clamor of daily living is ceased, you can hear a house talk in the stillness of the dark.

Our homes groan and creak as they settle into place. Parents padding around can make floorboards shift and squeak. Dripping faucets are amplified into heartbeats in the quiet of the night. Branches outside scratch and claw at windows when the breeze stirs. Heaters and boilers rev up with an ominous sound as if some great machine of doom is gearing up to do something awful. And God forbid if there's a shutter or gate that is loose, banging in the wind. Put it all together, and you have wide-eyed little ones pulling the sheets over their heads and wondering, "Can't anyone else hear all this scary stuff?"

I accidentally learned to embrace the night sounds.

Our neighbors let their kids roam wild on soft summer evenings long after I had to go to bed. I would press my nose to the screen, trying to catch a glimpse of what fun I was missing out on. Were they catching fireflies? Were they playing a spooky game of tag? And in the pauses of their running feet and laughter, I heard another sound. Deep, low, and mysterious.

With my nose pressed to the scratchy screen smelling of rusty metal and grass clippings, a different, deeper tone curled into my ear. Whoo-hoo-*hoooooo*. An owl! Or was it? I strained my ears, tuning out the neighborhood kids. Yes! There it was again, a hooting owl. I was thrilled.

The kids were too busy in their play to notice, so I fancied that I was the only one in our suburban block who noticed this serene visitor to our drowsy, tree-lined neighborhood. I wondered what else was out there that others were missing? Who else was out there talking in the night that most of us missed out on? Plenty.

Drawn to the exhalation of the carbon dioxide in my breath, the ubiquitous mosquitoes buzzed by my window. A few birds offered up brief, short trills. Frogs could be heard in the dense, wet, shrubby areas in early spring. Hot summers meant crickets chirping. On windy nights, I learned to relish the sound of wind hushing in the evergreens. And I loved storms. Cuddled under my blankets, a windy storm full of rain lashing at the windows was the perfect setting to read books.

Those experiences taught me that nature at night was magical and had its own music if you learned to listen.

We are never too old to learn to listen and train our

ears to a different sound. When my son started playing bass guitar, he and my husband helped me notice the bass playing in classical, rock, and jazz music. I began to discern the difference between a complicated combination of bass notes in a jazz performance and the boring one-note of some popular pop. I had never noticed bass before. It was always the melody, the top notes of the treble clef, that I could hear. But now I heard music with different ears.

It's the same with nature. We can train our ears to hear things, even if the neighbor's dog is barking. Even if we are unfamiliar with night sounds. Ears can be trained, just like you were potty trained.

As I grow older (and warmer), I usually sleep with the window open a bit. For one, I hate to be hot. More importantly, I like to drift asleep buoyed by the mysterious night sounds while tucked under my sheets.

I've discovered that wild turkeys really do make the "gobble-gobble" sound. But you're most likely to hear them at dawn. Because our poodle found a rabbit's nest one lazy summer afternoon, I know the hair-raising sound of rabbits screaming. So, when we rented a home next to a field, I could identify when a rabbit had been caught in the darkness of early morning. (It still made my skin crawl.)

I can identify the squeak of a bat (unfortunately). My father learned while camping next to a lake that the pounding and smacking noise he heard was beavers. They were slapping their broad tails against the water.

My sister lives on a rural property. One night while walking her dogs she heard an unearthly scream too close for comfort that had her riveted to the spot with all the hair on her neck standing straight up. We figured out later it was most likely a bobcat scream. They do that to frighten and paralyze their prey. Since bobcats are about the size of a miniature poodle and 30 pounds, I doubt that she was the prey that night. More likely, it was after a rabbit. And if you hear that scream from far away in the woods, it can sound like a woman in her death throes. Quite remarkable.

When I was thirteen and camping in Wisconsin, I heard a gorgeous trilling call that our camp counselor identified as a whip-poor-will bird. I've longed to hear it since, but because so much of its habitat of brush is no longer available (forests with sparse underbrush), it is not so common anymore. But the small, brown bird that likes to sleep on the ground has a captivating nighttime lullaby.

I can't identify all the calls, screams, snorts, and sounds of the night, but I enjoy tuning my ears for them. There's something deliciously enchanting and mysterious about witnessing this nighttime chorus of creatures.

One night, my husband and I were sleeping in our pop-up camper when I awoke to what seemed to be a chorus of cats mewling. I poked Tom and hissed, "What *is* that?" He sat up, listened for a bit, and muttered, "I'm pretty sure it's coyotes, " then fell back asleep.

Coyotes? That couldn't be! I imagined coyotes to sound like a lonesome wolf howl. This sounded too high-pitched, like a bunch of cats. Surely, coyotes would sound more like wolves—they're in the same family, after all. Clearly, he wasn't paying attention. I poked him again, "Are you sure? It sounds too high, like cats." He turned over and sighed, "Coyotes," and fell back asleep.

Later, I discovered that despite my bias on how I thought coyotes *should* sound, they do, in fact have a very high-pitched howl and sound nothing like the majestic wolf we see and hear in nature shows. I had doubted what I heard because I had assumed they sounded like their canine cousins. And I was also a little disappointed. What I *wanted* was a lonesome wolf howl. What it actually sounded like to me was a pack of cats. Or tiny, purse-fitting dogs. There was a gap between my expectations and reality. I think this happens when listening for God's voice as well.

Thanks to movies, books, or whatever media you glean it from, it seems that God should speak with a thundering voice. Waves should roar, mountains tremble, and our knees should quake if He ever deigns to talk to us. But that's not what the record shows. In fact, He's made it quite clear how we can hear from Him.

Although there are instances where God speaks in unusual ways, such as dreams (Joseph was urged to take Jesus away from Herod and into Egypt), angels (Sarah and Abraham to have a son although they were old), and loud voices (Paul on the road to Damascus) the usual way is the way that is most accessible to us—through His Word, the Bible.

In Romans chapter 10, we get a practical approach.

"How, then, can they call on the one they have not believed in? And how can they believe in the one of whom they have not heard? . . .Consequently, faith comes from hearing the message, and the message is heard through the word about Christ" (verses 14-17).

Most people could not read at that time, so they had to *hear* the message of the good news of freedom from sin. They had to be acquainted with and know God's words.

He made it quite clear to the Israelites wandering in the desert what His will was, having Moses write it down on tablets of stone.

So, although we may desire the thundering voice, an angel's appearance (and absolutely, He can choose to reveal Himself that way), or some unusual experience, to increase your odds of hearing from God, your best bet is to do two things:

Shut off other voices (put down your phone).

Read His Word.

What do I mean to shut off other voices? Well, when I've heard God most clearly, it's been because I'm alone and quiet. I may be walking outside or lying on my pillow at night, but there are no other competitors for my attention. I'm not listening to music or a podcast. I'm enveloped in silence (except for the chatter in my head).

Familiarity with God's Word gives you the best opportunity to hear His voice. He will *never* communicate something contrary to His Word. So, if someone says to you, "I heard a voice telling me to pull the trigger on that guy," that is entirely contrary to the commandment, "Thou shall not kill." He may have heard a voice, but it wasn't God.

God's word is powerful for giving us strength, direction, wisdom, and peace. When Jesus was challenged by Satan, He did what any of us can do: He spoke the Word of God. And Satan (who can't stand to be in the presence of Truth) stop harassing Him and left.

If you want to get to know someone well, your spouse or a friend, you learn to speak their language. My father's family comes from Norway, so when he was disgusted or felt something was repugnant, he would say, "Uff da!"

Meaning, *ewwww*. If you're from the South and you don't want to say that someone's effort fell short, you don't say, "Well, she bombed that attempt." You say, "Well, bless her heart." It's a backhanded way of saying, "She failed, but she tried." If you know the language, you know what they are saying.

So, if you're familiar with the language of God, you'll know it when He speaks to you. And the result will be an immediate sense of peace.

An example of this is what happened to me in the middle of a book signing. I was at a party for a friend's book on cancer when I began talking with one of the survivors. She told me that she didn't believe that things like cancer passed through God's hands or that He was involved. Things like that happening to us were just random in her opinion. Unbeknownst to her, that started off a roaring tumult in my mind.

I might have stood there with a frozen smile, but I couldn't hear her anymore. It was like I was in the doctor's office hearing news I couldn't accept, couldn't reconcile, my brain couldn't receive because it was so scary.

I was amid a seven-year struggle with infertility. I had been to many doctors and had endured many procedures. I needed to know that God was intimately familiar with all this and was in control. If not, that meant I was just out here swinging in the wind completely alone. It meant that I had to figure out all the science and technology on my own with my limited brain. I felt this sense of despair and panic wash over me. Feelings of drowning, hopelessness, and fear swirled around me. It was like the roaring of a monster storm. It blotted out everything else she was saying and anyone else there. It was just me in the eye of that awful storm.

Then, very quietly, it felt like these words were whispered in my ear: "I know the hairs on your head." Immediately, everything stilled. All was quiet, and a tremendous sense of peace and confidence washed over me. Why? Because those were the words of Jesus. In Matthew 10:30, He told the disciples that He knew them intimately—He knew the hairs on their heads. That even when a sparrow falls, He knows. Clearly, the Holy Spirit was reminding me of the truth: I was not alone. He was involved and in control.

If I hadn't known those words, I couldn't have discerned who was speaking to me or what they were saying. You don't have to memorize the Bible. But familiarity with parables, promises, and points that God's Word gives us allows His Holy Spirit to use what we know to speak words of truth and peace when we need them.

When you can discern God's voice,
you remove a lot of choice.

When you can discern God's voice, you remove a lot of choice. Meaning, we can remove a lot of dodgy decisions, perilous paths, and idiotic ideas about who He is and what He wants for us. Your choice is simplified: believe His Word and live it, or not.

Learning to listen to night sounds will help you learn to listen for God's still, small voice. He doesn't shout. He doesn't shame. He never bullies. He murmurs, He cajoles,

He invites. And we can decide whether to tune in or not. We can decide whether to get familiar with His language or not. After several teachings on His parables, Jesus ended with, "he who has ears to hear, let him (or her) hear" (Mark 4:9).

It may be in the middle of the night, while on a walk, or a lonely moment in the middle of a party, but learning to quiet the clatter and clamor in your head and listen to the sounds of silence can bring you God's very presence and peace. No matter how dark your night.

Moonlit Musings

1. What night sounds do you know and like? It could be rain on the roof, cows mooing, owls hooting or crickets.

2. Try making a list of things to listen for in the silence—insects buzzing, wind in the trees, birdsong, rain, icy branches clacking together, squeaky snow underfoot, the crunch of fall leaves, waves from a lake, a frozen lake cracking under pressure, frogs at night, crickets, rivulets in a stream, crashing seas, water lapping at stones or shells, waterfalls. . .or more!

3. What situations could you create to foster the "still, small voice" of God? Could it be biblical truth in a song? Spending time with a wise friend? A quiet walk outside? Time spent memorizing verses?

4. Have you ever been in a situation where you couldn't hear others because of the storm in your mind? What verse could you memorize to combat that confusion and dread?

Prayer

Heavenly Father,

Thank you for the magic and mystery of the night. The hooting of owls, howling of coyotes, and chorus of crickets is a lovely symphony of your creation. Please help me to learn and remember your Word—the calls of contentment, the promise of peace, the wisdom for my way. Recall to my mind your promises to always be there for me when I'm overwhelmed.

In Jesus' name, amen.

CHAPTER 22

Moon

T he bright light caught the corner of my eye, and I looked up. There, 25 feet up in the living room window, peeked the moon. It was making its nightly trip through the dark—just above the tree line—and across our windows. Later, I would see it around 3 a.m. for my usual bathroom break after it rounded the corner of the house to beam into our bedroom windows. Like a benign, old friend, it resolutely covered the same path each night. Month after month, it appears to morph and change its shape, but is always there. Making the dark not so impenetrable with its pock-marked, shining, benevolent face.

Some nights it shines so brightly on our pillows that it wakes us up. I alternate between wanting to greet it with, "Well, helllooo there!" and wanting to pull my pillow over my head to shut out its penetrating light.

On inky nights of a scuba dive or navigating steps in the dark, I'm happy to see it shining in the sky and illuminating the landscape around me. At 3 a.m., when it wakes me up? Not so much. But sometimes, I stop on my way to the bathroom in the quiet of night and marvel at our faithful, celestial companion.

Terms like "gibbous" and "waxing" versus "waning" drift through my half-conscious mind. Why do they call it the "new moon" when you can't see it? Wouldn't a "new moon" be shiny and new? At what point is it gibbous vs. crescent? (And who made up that term "gibbous" anyhow?) It sounds like the call of gibbering, evil monkeys of the night. Not our warm, benevolent watchman and darkness illuminator.

Because it is part of the night, the moon has always enchanted us. We've built up myths, mysteries, and stories about this changing celestial body that rules the dark hours of our days.

Hospital nurses will swear that things get busier and crazier during a full moon despite research saying it's a myth. Gardeners will tell you to plant seedlings during a waxing moon (as it's getting brighter) rather than a waning moon for successful gardens. Stories about vampires and werewolves revolve around the moon phases. And every woman of childbearing age is acutely aware of the moon's influence over her body.

Since time began, we are enchanted by the moon. Our ancestors looked up into the heavenly realms sprinkled with galaxies and wondered at the moon's changes and impact on us.

Around the world, we made up stories to help us understand the moon's changing visage and ethereal beauty.

In Chinese culture, the moon looms large. They have a major festival called the Moon Festival—or Mid-Autumn Festival—held on a full moon, of course. Its popularity is similar to the Chinese New Year. During this festival, people carry lanterns of different shapes and sizes, which symbolize the light for people's path to prosperity and good fortune. Mooncakes, a rich pastry usually filled with sweet bean, egg yolk, meat, or lotus-seed pods, are traditionally eaten during this time. Families make great efforts to come together, often traveling enormous distances, to celebrate being together with family and eating moon cakes. (Sort of like Americans mad scramble to be home for Thanksgiving). It all stems from the folktale about Chang'e.

While there are several variations on the tale of Chang'e, the gist of it is this:

Chang'e was an exceptionally beautiful woman. Ten firey suns had risen above the Earth and scorched it with their blazing heat—causing misery and hardship for the people. Hou Yi, Chang'e's husband, was a famous archer who shot down nine of the ten suns, leaving just one sun in the sky. For this, he was rewarded with two portions of the elixir of immortality. Since he did not want to gain immortality without his wife, he left both portions in her keeping for the day when they would take it. One day, he went off hunting for food, and his apprentice broke into his house and tried to force Chang'e to give him the elixir. Chang'e swallowed both portions herself rather than give them up to the apprentice.

Up, up she flew to the heavens, and chose the moon for her immortal residence since she loved her husband and wanted to be near him. When Hou Yi discovered what had happened, he displayed the fruits and cakes his wife loved, then killed himself.

However, older versions of this tale say that Chang'e stole the elixir from her husband, drank it, and flew to the moon so her husband could not go after her. Readers' choice, I guess!

The Native Americans were a little more practical than the Chinese when it came to observing and respecting the moon's phases.

In Native American mythology, the moon is a guardian spirit, guide, timekeeper, and protector associated with transformation. The moon also represents the natural rhythms of the environment, which often dictates activities like planting, hunting, and celebration.

I've been confused about the moon's actual activities for a while. Maybe I wasn't paying attention in school. But I erroneously assumed some things. Myths such as:

- The moon spins as we do, and that's why we see different amounts of light on it.
- The phases of the moon are different around the world (If it's a full moon here, it must be a new moon over the Indian Ocean, which is directly opposite the United States on the globe.)
- The shadowed part of the moon is due to the Earth casting its shadow.

All of these assumptions are false. And for those who were paying attention in basic astronomy classes, the following facts will be obvious and boring to you. But I don't mind admitting ignorance, so here are some facts on the moon and its properties.

First of all, NASA has a great, simple video showing how

the moon orbits our Earth. You can find it here: https:// science.nasa.gov/moon/moon-phases/.

And those weird terms? As you see in the illustration below, they are (in order): 1-new moon, 2-waxing crescent, 3-first quarter, 4-waxing gibbous, 5-full, 6-waning gibbous, 7-last quarter, 8-waning crescent, new moon (again).

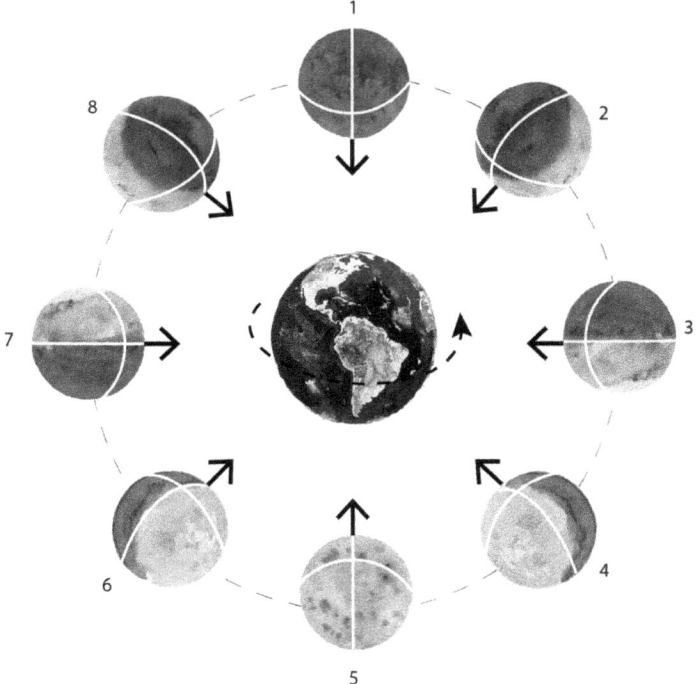

Diagram is not to scale. Arrows on moon indicate the face that we see.

Waxing refers to the moon as getting fuller, brighter, and bigger to our eyes. I think of it as being like how they used to make candles. Repeatedly dipping tapered (long) candles into the hot wax mixture gradually coats them and makes them bigger. Waning is the opposite. The brightness is getting smaller to our eyes. And the term "gibbous?" That is when more than half of the moon is illuminated. That's between quarter and full. Gibbous is the Latin word for "hump" and has been used for centuries to describe rounded or convex shapes.

The Creator of Heaven and Earth surely understands the phases of the moon, its gravitational pull, and how it orbits around our planet in synchronicity as we orbit and spin around the sun. But, curiously, the Bible doesn't mention that. It seems to God that these facts are not important for our spiritual development and getting to know Him better. Meaning, all we are told is that He made the moon to give us light in the night. There is no mention of gravitational pull, tidal changes, or how plants and people react to its forces.

The movement of the celestial bodies has always confused me. I know the Earth takes a full year to travel around the sun. But the moon? What exactly is it doing? If we are spinning and orbiting and we see it in the night sky, it must be too. It seems like it is spinning as we do, isn't that why it changes in the amount of light we see? But I was wrong.

While Earth spins a complete circle every 24 hours and at the same time orbits around the sun in a calendar year, the moon behaves differently. The moon travels (orbits) around our globe—much like we do around the sun—but it is, unlike us, *not spinning. The same side of the moon always faces us.* No matter if it's a crescent moon barely reflecting much of the sun's light or a full moon fully reflecting the sun's light. We never see the back side or the dark side of the moon. The same side always faces us as it circles around our Earth in about a month. And so, everyone on Earth always sees the same full moon within a few hours of each other.

You'll notice in the above paragraph I resort to the word "always" a lot. I like that surety about how the world works. We *always* circle around the sun. It *always takes* a full year. We *always* complete a full 360° spin on our axis in about 24 hours as we orbit the sun over the course of a year. The moon *always orbits* around us (while we are going around the sun) in about 29 days and *always* has the same side facing us. In a world where truth seems malleable, much is changeable, and things and people that promised always to be there but frequently fail, these *always* facts about God's creation provide surety, substance, and reliability of the forces at work around us.

And although the *always* in science bring me comfort, there are still some unknowables. Like, why doesn't the moon spin during its orbit around us? The Earth spins, so why not the moon? But the Bible is not a science book. The Bible is a book on relationships. And the primary lesson God wants to convey to us is that He is *always* about relationships.

He wants us to know that He is *always* in control. He *always* knows what's going on everywhere. He *always* inclines His ear to us. He *always* desires us to draw closer. He and the heavenly host *always* rejoice when we turn from our wanderings back to Him. *Always.*

This is in contrast to the stories we make up or tell ourselves about Him. We are not so far from prehistoric people gazing up at the moon and making up versions about what our mysterious God is like. Or maybe we've been told these lies and myths through literature or well-meaning religious people. For example:

Myth: "God certainly has more important things to attend to in the world than listen to me."
Truth: He wants to hear from you.

"Cast all your anxiety on him because he cares for you" (1 Peter 5:7).

Myth: "I have to go through a priest, pastor, or saint to talk to God. I can't approach Him directly."
Truth: You are welcome as you are; no mediator is needed.

"So whenever we are in need, we should come bravely before the throne of our merciful God. There we will be treated with undeserved grace, and we will find help" (Hebrews 4:16 CEV). And, "There is one God, and one mediator between God and mankind, the man Christ Jesus. . ." (1 Timothy 2:5).

Myth: "I've been so horrible, I'm sure I need to do some sort of penance or clean up my life, so I'm sure He doesn't want to hear from me."
Truth: He has already paid the price—or made you clean—the way is open to you. Come as you are!

"What then shall we say to these things? If God is for us, who can be against us? He who did not spare His own Son, but gave him up for us all, how will he not also with him graciously give us all things? Who shall bring any charge against God's elect? It is God who justifies. . .No, in all these things we are more than conquerors through him who loved us. For I am sure that neither death nor life, nor angels nor rulers, nor things present nor things to come, nor powers, nor height nor depth, nor anything else in all creation, will be able to separate us from the love of God in Christ Jesus our Lord" (Romans 8:31-39 ESV).

Myth: "It's so difficult to hear God; besides, who am I that He would want to communicate with me?"
Truth: "The Lord is close to the brokenhearted and saves those who are crushed in spirit" (Psalm 34:18).

Like prehistoric people, we make up all sorts of stories about the invisible and omnipotent God we feel is so distant from us. We know He's there, but He feels far off. But unlike the moon, which is about 239 thousand miles away, God is not far off from us. He's as close as our nearest breath, "The Lord is near to all who call on Him, to all who call on Him in truth" (Psalm 145:18 NIV). And there's no mystery about how to draw closer to Him. "Draw near to God, and he will draw near to you" (James 4:8 ESV).

※※・※※

If we want God to feel near,
we need to drop our myths and fears.

※※・※※

Perhaps we feel like God is thousands of miles away due to our first experiences of attachment. In the 1970s, Harvard professor Ed Tronick published the results of the Still Face experiment that demonstrated the devastating effects of lack of attachment or lack of a warm reception by our primary caregivers.

In the experiment, a mother warmly responded to her

baby in a high chair. They interacted, touched hands, and giggled and laughed. Then the mother turned away and turned back to her child with a still, unresponsive face. The child was confused, distraught, and tried unsuccessfully to get a response from her mother's indifferent Still Face. Eventually, the child withered, fell apart sobbing, and slumped defeated in her chair. When the mother reengaged with her transformed warm face, the wary child took a while to warm up. This experience was repeated with older toddlers with the same result.

We psychologically, biologically, and spiritually need to have a warm, receptive face to our attempts at interaction. Is it any wonder as we "interact" more and more through computers and walk amongst Still Faces in our cities that we are suffering from anxiety, loneliness, and other signs of disordered and unmet attachments? We are designed to connect with others. Whether Still Face happens to you as an infant, as a teenager from peers or family, or in adulthood, it leaves a painful wound. (And can we agree that parents with their faces glued to their phones is another form of Still Face to children?) Blessedly, God's Word assures us we can expect a warm face, not a Still Face, when we reach out to Him.

In the middle of the night when I can't sleep, I try to pray for others. It helps my problems diminish when I consider a list of loved ones who need my prayers or could benefit from a little lift in their spirits. And all the while, as the moon is beaming light on me through my window, it reminds me that God's face is always shining towards me, always beholding me, never turning away. No matter what my behavior or my struggles may be. No matter what my dark thoughts tell me. I know He's quietly beaming love to me, no matter where I am on the Earth. And it's true for you, too. He is beholding you with quiet, receptive light to help you through the night.

In our darkest nights, amongst our deepest fears, God's benevolent face of love—like the moon—is *always turned towards you.* It is in our myths, lies, and fears that we think this is not so.

And His Son—like the moon—always reflects God's light towards us, never turning away. Even though we can't see it during a new moon, it's still there. This gives me hope and surety that although my feelings may say God is distant, He is not. He is there. Through our spinning and changing ways, through our navigating a myriad of Still Faces, through our stumbling and staggering through the darkness, He is always *facing toward us.* Always wanting us to draw closer.

Always.

Moonlit Musings

1. Have you ever believed—or told yourself—the myths about God's reception of you?
2. Has there been anyone in your life who always received you with warmth and acceptance? (Could be a coach, teacher, relative, or spouse, for example.)
3. When in your life have you experienced Still Face from others?
4. Which of the verses mentioned impacted you the most on how God regards you?

Prayer

Heavenly Father,

What a relief it is to know you always face me with a warm, receptive face! In a world of Still Faces, you are not. Help me to receive these truths about who you are, and how much you love me. Show me where I might be clinging to old myths in contrast to what your Word says. Illuminate to me where I might be showing a Still Face to people in my family and community. Thank you for your constancy and love.

In Jesus' name, amen.

Acknowledgements

I would like to thank my husband Tom who initially picked this book idea from a list and said, "That one." Thanks, sweetie, for always believing in me, encouraging me, and bathing me in Truth (even when I don't like it). And thank you for keeping the window open at night!

Thanks also to my late-night companion and sharp-eyed editor, my son Jack. If there's a needle in a haystack, he's your guy.

As ever, thanks to my writing group beta readers: Pat Sikora, Stephanie Shoquist, and Darla Bennett. Thanks also to Kari Clauson who provided feedback.

Heartfelt gratitude to my editor Arnetta from lineup-onlineservices.com. Your enthusiasm and excitement over this book kept me going when I had feelings of, "Why am I even bothering? Who cares?"

Special thanks to beta reader Lynne Hurrell (see Beaver chapter). As well as being a fashion diva and always ready for company, Lynne reads more books than anyone I know and produces thoughtful and excellent feedback. She also has the best, deep, throaty guffaw when laughing. (And if you fall on the pickleball court and break both your wrists, she's perfect in an emergency. Thanks Lynne!)

Finally, unspeakable gratitude to the Creator of this beautiful world who crammed it so full of heartbreaking delight, it brings me to tears. What an honor to introduce others to your wonders!

> *"Earth's crammed with heaven,*
> *And every common bush afire with God."*
> *- Elizabeth Barrett Browning*

Looking for more?

You can find free resources about Nature at Night (audio sleep help, downloadable bookmarks, scripture cards and art) at:

LaurieKehler.com/nightresources

May these resources help you face the dark with wonder, confidence in your Creator, and peace in your heart.

If you'd like to buy nature-themed gifts like mugs, cards and tshirts, you can see them at:

TheNatureOfHopeShop.com

More books by Laurie Kehler

This Outside Life - Finding God in the Heart of Nature

Gardening Mercies - Finding God in Your Garden

Wings of Mercy - Spiritual Reflections from
the Birds of the Air

To *listen to Laurie's podcasts visit,*
The Nature of Hope
And,
This Outside Life
on your favorite podcast platform.

For a deluxe, *color* edition of this book, please visit:

www.ingramcontent.com/pod-product-compliance
Lightning Source LLC
Chambersburg PA
CBHW051614120626
46551CB00014B/1784